THE
PREPPER'S
WORKBOOK

CHECKLISTS, WORKSHEETS *and* HOME PROJECTS
to PROTECT YOUR FAMILY *from* ANY DISASTER

Sc

This book is the private property of: _____

If found, please return to: _____

• • •

Published in the U.S. by
ULYSSES PRESS
P.O. Box 3440
Berkeley, CA 94703
www.ulyssespress.com

ISBN: 978-1-61243-226-7
Library of Congress Control Number 2013938629

Printed in the United States by Bang Printing

10 9 8 7 6 5 4 3 2 1

Acquisitions Editor: Keith Riegert
Managing Editor: Claire Chun
Editor: Lauren Harrison
Front cover design: Jenna Stempel
Interior design and layout: Jake Flaherty
Photo credits: see page 199

Distributed by Publishers Group West

NOTE TO READERS: This book is independently authored and published and no sponsorship or endorsement of this book by, and no affiliation with, any trademarked product mentioned or pictured within is claimed or suggested. All trademarks that appear in the text, illustrations or photographs in this book belong to their respective owners and are used here for informational purposes only. The authors and publisher encourage readers to patronize the recommended products mentioned and pictured in this book. This book has been written and published strictly for informational purposes, and in no way should be used as a substitute for actual instruction with qualified professionals. The authors and publisher are providing you with information in this work so that you can have the knowledge and can choose, at your own risk, to act on that knowledge. The authors and publisher also urge all readers to be aware of their health status, to consult local fish and game laws, and to consult health care and outdoor professionals before engaging in any potentially hazardous activity. Any use of the information in this book is made on the reader's good judgment. The author and publisher assume no liability for personal injury to the reader or others harmed by the reader, property damage, consequential damage or loss, however caused, from using the information in this book.

Contents

- - - - - - - - -

Foreword

- - - - - - - - -

I first became acquainted with Scott Williams by reading *Bug Out: The Complete Plan for Escaping a Catastrophic Disaster Before It's Too Late*. This was the first of his books I'd read and to say I was impressed is a dramatic understatement. Here was a guy who'd truly been there and done that. Not only did he have practical experience, he was able to communicate his knowledge effectively. His writing style was easy to follow and a pleasure to the eyes and mind.

Time and again in subsequent books, Scott has shown he is no armchair prepper. His knowledge and skills have been hard-won by doing rather than just reading a few books and regurgitating the same information someone else came up with and never tested in the real world.

I'd hazard a guess and say that well over 90 percent of preppers are list makers. We make lists of bug-out bag contents, food pantry supplies (both what we have on hand and what we need to acquire), wish lists of the gear we'd love to buy once we get that bonus from work, to-do lists for chores and projects. The list of lists goes on and on, doesn't it?

That said, many preppers, even the ones who have been around a while, are probably missing a thing or two (or more) on those lists. Maybe they forgot about them, maybe they never heard of them before. No matter the case, more than one prepper has agonized over whether they've accounted for everything. When the balloon goes up, or the grid goes down, is the worst possible time to realize you forgot something.

The beauty of *The Prepper's Workbook* is they've done the remembering for you. With easy-to-understand forms and checklists, all you need to do is fill in the blanks. Granted, that might be oversimplifying things just a tad as prepping in general involves (or should involve) a lot more doing than reading. The point is, follow the proverbial bouncing ball and, by the end, you should be fairly well set should disaster strike.

I know many preppers who are avid readers and they often lament a creased cover or a dog-eared page as they want to keep the books looking as nice as they can. This book, however, is made to be beaten up, written in, marked up with highlighters. If at the end of the day it looks like a five-year-old college textbook, with all sorts of notes in the margins, then you've used the book correctly.

Every prepper has a different plan for what to do in a crisis and how to go about getting things done. That's as it should be as we each face unique circumstances and challenges. There is no one single game plan that will work for everyone. That is where *The Prepper's Workbook* will really help, as it allows for customization to suit your individual needs, strengths and weaknesses. By following the instructions and filling out the forms, you will be able to create a survival plan that is unique and perfectly suited for you and your family.

Fill out the worksheets, run through the checklists, complete the projects. Take your time and do everything the way it should be done—no cheating! Be honest with yourself and recognize where your plan is lacking, then work toward improving on that weakness.

Even if the worst never comes to pass and you never have the opportunity to truly put your plans to the test, you'll rest easier at night knowing that if the world begins to fall apart in the morning, you're ready for it.

—Jim Cobb
    Author of *Prepper's Home Defense* and
    The Prepper's Complete Book of Disaster Readiness

Introduction:
HOW TO USE THIS WORKBOOK

As the title implies, *The Prepper's Workbook* is an interactive workbook and not the kind of book you read passively for entertainment or to glean bits and pieces information that might soon be forgotten. This book is all about you and your family, and is designed to enable you to be better prepared for any kind of disaster or emergency survival situation. And although we use the word "prepper" in the title, this is not just another book for those expecting a major doomsday event or upheaval of society. By definition, a "prepper" is someone who prepares in advance for any change in normal circumstances. Such a change may be as short-lived as an overnight power outage caused by an electrical storm, or it could be an extended collapse of the grid caused by major natural or manmade disasters.

Disasters typically happen with little or no warning and leave in their wake the ill prepared who will inevitably suffer for their lack or readiness or become reliant upon others for their most basic needs and comforts. To avoid becoming such a victim, you must begin the process of preparedness now. *The Prepper's Workbook* will help you do that by providing you with worksheets, checklists and activities that you can customize to fit your particular circumstances, including your geographical location and your family's living situation, whether it is in the city or the country, in an apartment or a house.

To get the most out of this book, you will need to actively participate in the exercises suggested and take the time to fill in the blanks on the pages requiring vital information, lists and maps. Doing this properly may take some time, and that's okay. The important thing is to start. As you go along, you will work your way through the book and have the great satisfaction of knowing that you have taken the first steps toward preparing yourself and your family for safety and survival.

To begin, it is important to go through the exercises in the first chapter of this book. These exercises are all about getting yourself and your home organized, assessing your surroundings and the threats that could affect you and your family, and taking stock of what you already have on hand that may be useful in an emergency. In this chapter you will also map the vital locations in the nearby area outside of your home, so that everyone in your family will know how to find the nearest emergency services and other critical locations without having to try to look this up under duress.

Moving beyond the beginning organizational section, *The Prepper's Workbook* takes you step by step through preparing to shelter in place in the home. Flowcharts to help you assess the viability of sheltering in place or the necessity to bug out and evacuate are also provided. If you do have to leave your home, the sections on how to build a bug-out bag, equip a bug-out vehicle and decide where to go will make you much more prepared than those who leave in a panic with no real plan.

Beyond these preliminary steps, the remainder of this workbook deals with specific types of threats and how to determine if they may affect you, and if so, how to prepare for them. The final chapter covers the Prepping Top Tens, outlining ten vital survival skills everyone should know and practice in advance of needing them in a real emergency.

USING INDIVIDUAL SECTIONS AND WORKSHEETS

INFORMATIONAL WORKSHEETS

The informational worksheets in each chapter are designed to give you a physical, hard copy of vital information for each member of your family all in one place—in this book. With today's over-reliance on storing personal information and contacts in computers and smartphones, these worksheets are essential. Fill in as many details as you feel comfortable with, and keep the book in a safe place.

CHECKLISTS

You will find a ton of helpful checklists in this book—they are essential for making sure you have everything you need to be fully prepared. However, there is no single checklist of preparedness equipment and supplies that can meet the needs of every family. Your specific needs may be unique to your geographical location, family member needs and personal situation. So, with each standard checklist worksheet we provide, we also provide the space for you to build your own custom checklist or to add items as you see fit. Your main goal is to fully prepare for your own family, and when it comes to that, you're the one who knows best. We're just getting you started in the right direction.

MAPS, CHARTS AND DIAGRAMS

The maps, charts and diagrams that this book asks you complete are designed to ensure that everyone in the household is able to find critical items and places both inside and out of the house, whether that's locating the fuse box, first aid kit or closest evacuation center. Like the personal information you collect in the informational worksheets, these maps are meant to break the dependence on electronic information. Google Maps may be a great way to find your nearest fire station, but it's all for naught if the power has been out for five days. Beyond the walls of your home, the maps you provide will familiarize everyone in your family with the surrounding environment and locations they may need to know in a crisis. These do-it-yourself illustrations do not have to be elaborate or artistic—you should feel free to print out maps from online or collect them from your local AAA office, and charts and diagrams can be simple sketches—the important thing is that they convey accurate information.

ACTIVITIES

Throughout each chapter, you'll also find activities. These are suggestions for hands-on projects to better prepare your home, vehicles and other equipment, as well as hone your personal and family's survival skills. They range from simple projects like crafting a 24-hour survival kit for your car to weekend projects like building storm shutters for your home and quick skills drills like practicing a flood evacuation. Most of these activities are designed to be affordable, quick and easy, but not all of them will be applicable to every family, so choose the ones only that apply to your area and your needs.

PREPPER'S TIPS & TRICKS

Throughout the pages of these book you will find extra tips, tricks and interesting tidbits of information that both of us have picked up from decades of survival training and practical use. They range from facts about disasters to practical prepping cheats that can help you stay safe and comfortable.

Now that you know this is not a book to kick back with for armchair entertainment, it's time to roll up our sleeves and get started putting the "work" in *The Prepper's Workbook*.

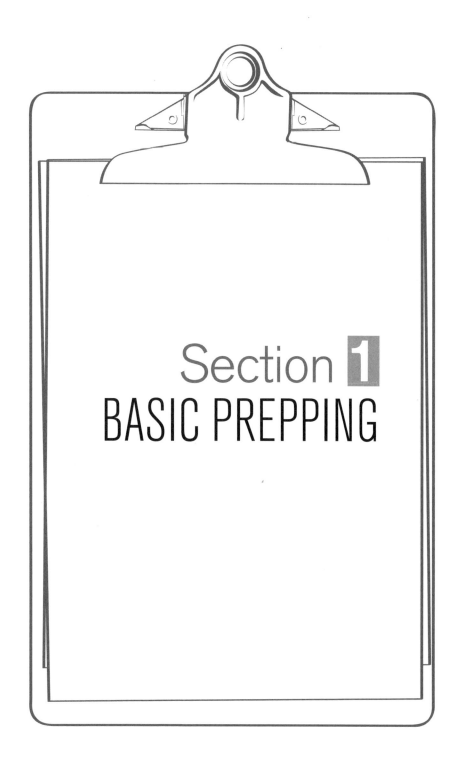

Section 1
BASIC PREPPING

Chapter 1:
GETTING STARTED

ORGANIZING YOUR FAMILY INFORMATION

The first step in preparing yourself and your family for an emergency is to get organized and gather detailed, vital information for each member of the family and put it all in one place (in the Family Member Information pages that follow) so you and everyone else in your household will have access to it. This information includes medical details like blood type, required medications and known allergies, but also personal details such as Social Security Numbers and even contact info.

With today's dependence upon technology, such as smartphones that store numbers and e-mail addresses that can be accessed with one touch or even a voice command, it's not surprising that many people no longer commit to memory the phone numbers of even their closest loved ones. If you don't know your wife's or husband's phone number by heart, you're certainly not alone, but now is the time to change those habits, and even if you can't memorize contact info for everyone in your family, you can certainly write it down on the pages that follow.

Having this detailed information in one place could be one of the most valuable parts of your prepping if you or one of your family members is injured or turns up missing in a catastrophe. You should fill in as much or as little information as you'd like. Just remember, each piece of information in this chapter could prove invaluable if you and your loved ones are separated during a disaster.

ACTIVITY 1.1: **EMERGENCY CONTACTS**

This exercise consists of two activities. First, you'll write down your family's outside emergency contacts so that you have them all in one place. Second, you'll create individual, business card–sized contact cards that everyone in your family should carry with them on their person.

OUTSIDE EMERGENCY CONTACT SHEET

Name: _____

Home Phone: _____ Work Phone: _____

Cell Phone: _____

E-mail: _____

Mailing Address: _____

_____

Name: _____

Home Phone: _____ Work Phone: _____

Cell Phone: _____

E-mail: _____

Mailing Address: _____

_____

Name: _____

Home Phone: _____ Work Phone: _____

Cell Phone: _____

E-mail: _____

Mailing Address: _____

_____

Name: _____

Home Phone: _____ Work Phone: _____

Cell Phone: _____

E-mail: _____

Mailing Address: _____

_____

CONTACT CARDS

These cards are meant to be carried on the person of each of your immediate family members. Stick them in a backpack, purse or wallet, if anyone ever loses their phone, this single piece of paper could save the day.

> **Emergency Contacts**
> John Smith: (h) 917-555-9091 (w) 212-555-8811
> Deb. Smith: (m) 917-555-2209 (w) 212-555-7172
>
> Dr. Carl Johnson (doctor): (m) 917-555-8877
> Patricia Jones (aunt): (m) 415-555-0918
> Henry Smith (grandfather): (h) 606-555-7100
> Bill Harris (work): (w) 212-555-8813

Construct by hand:

1. Take a sheet of thick card stock.

2. Cut the card into 2x3-inch pieces.

3. Using a small-tipped permanent marker (that won't run when wet) print the following information on both sides of the card:

Immediate Contact #1	Name and Phone Number(s)	(wife/husband/father/mother)
Immediate Contact #2	Name and Phone Number(s)	(wife/husband/father/mother)
Outside Contact #1	Name and Phone Number(s)	(sibling/relative/friend/coworker)
Outside Contact #2	Name and Phone Number(s)	(sibling/relative/friend/coworker)
Outside Contact #3	Name and Phone Number(s)	(sibling/relative/friend/coworker)

Construct by computer:

1. Print the information above on regular paper, carefully sizing the font so it fits within 2x3 inches.

2. Using a photocopier (no ink to rub off or run when wet), copy the information onto a sheet of thick card stock.

3. Cut the card into 2x3-inch pieces.

ACTIVITY 1.2: FAMILY MEMBER INFORMATION

These detailed family member information sheets could become critical during or after a disaster, especially if one or more members of the family are injured or incapacitated, or if family members become separated.

TIPS & TRICKS

GET THE FAMILY ON BOARD

It's likely that not every member of your family will share your enthusiasm for preparedness planning, especially in the beginning. If you have a reluctant spouse or children, it is important to find prepping-related activities they can get excited about without dwelling on doom and disaster. Family camping trips or other small adventures utilizing similar checklists, supplies and equipment are a good start.

FAMILY MEMBER INFORMATION SHEET

Full legal name: _____

Date of birth: _____

Place of birth: _____

Height: _____

Weight: _____

Eye color: _____

Hair color: _____

Physical description: _____

_____

_____

_____

Address: _____

_____

_____

Phone number: _____

E-mail: _____

SSN (optional): _____

PASTE PHOTO HERE

Date of photo: _____

Fingerprints/DNA sample (optional)

Personal Medical Information

Primary doctor: _____

Phone: _____ Blood type: _____

Allergies: _____

Medical conditions: _____

_____

_____

Medications: _____

_____

_____

Notes: _____

FAMILY MEMBER INFORMATION SHEET

Full legal name: _____

Date of birth: _____

Place of birth: _____

Height: _____

Weight: _____

Eye color: _____

Hair color: _____

Physical description:_____

_____

_____

_____

Address: _____

_____

_____

Phone number: _____

E-mail: _____

SSN (optional): _____

PASTE PHOTO HERE

Date of photo: _____

Fingerprints/DNA sample (optional)

Personal Medical Information

Primary doctor: _____

Phone: _____ Blood type: _____

Allergies: _____

Medical conditions: _____

_____

_____

Medications: _____

_____

_____

Notes: _____

FAMILY MEMBER INFORMATION SHEET

Full legal name: _____

Date of birth: _____

Place of birth: _____

Height: _____

Weight: _____

Eye color: _____

Hair color: _____

Physical description: _____

_____

_____

_____

Address: _____

_____

_____

Phone number: _____

E-mail: _____

SSN (optional): _____

PASTE
PHOTO
HERE

Date of photo: _____

Fingerprints/DNA sample (optional)

Personal Medical Information

Primary doctor: _____

Phone: _____ Blood type: _____

Allergies: _____

Medical conditions: _____

_____

_____

Medications: _____

_____

_____

Notes: _____

FAMILY MEMBER INFORMATION SHEET

Full legal name: _____

Date of birth: _____

Place of birth: _____

Height: _____

Weight: _____

Eye color: _____

Hair color: _____

Physical description: _____

_____

_____

_____

PASTE
PHOTO
HERE

Date of photo: _____

Fingerprints/DNA sample (optional)

Address: _____

_____

_____

Phone number: _____

E-mail: _____

SSN (optional): _____

Personal Medical Information

Primary doctor: _____

Phone: _____ Blood type: _____

Allergies: _____

Medical conditions: _____

_____

_____

Medications: _____

_____

_____

Notes: _____

FAMILY MEMBER INFORMATION SHEET

Full legal name: _____

Date of birth: _____

Place of birth: _____

Height: _____

Weight: _____

Eye color: _____

Hair color: _____

Physical description: _____

_____

_____

_____

Address: _____

_____

_____

Phone number: _____

E-mail: _____

SSN (optional): _____

PASTE PHOTO HERE

Date of photo: _____

Fingerprints/DNA sample (optional)

Personal Medical Information

Primary doctor: _____

Phone: _____ Blood type: _____

Allergies: _____

Medical conditions: _____

_____

_____

Medications: _____

_____

_____

Notes: _____

FAMILY MEMBER INFORMATION SHEET

Full legal name: _____

Date of birth: _____

Place of birth: _____

Height: _____

Weight: _____

Eye color: _____

Hair color: _____

Physical description: _____

_____

_____

_____

Address: _____

_____

_____

Phone number: _____

E-mail: _____

SSN (optional): _____

PASTE
PHOTO
HERE

Date of photo: _____

Fingerprints/DNA sample (optional)

Personal Medical Information

Primary doctor: _____

Phone: _____   Blood type: _____

Allergies: _____

Medical conditions: _____

_____

_____

Medications: _____

_____

_____

Notes: _____

AN OBSESSION WITH CHECKLISTS

As adventure travelers, sea kayakers and offshore sailors, as well as authors, we are both obsessed with checklists out of long habit, and it was this obsession that led to the conception of this book. When you are about to set off into a trackless wilderness or cast off the dock lines for a passage on the high seas, forgetting some critical piece of equipment can be a matter of life or death. Disasters can quickly put anyone at any time in a similar situation, where going to the store to pick up what you forgot is not an option.

TAKING STOCK OF YOUR STOCK

Now that you've recorded vital information on who you are making emergency preparations for, it's time to do a realistic assessment of what you already have on hand so you know where you stand at the beginning. The following is a checklist for the basic necessities for surviving your average natural disaster. Before diving too deep into this book, check to see how many of these elemental supplies and emergency items you already have on hand now. In the chapters that follow, discussions and worksheets will help you make sure you haven't overlooked anything essential and that you have enough of everything in each category for every member of your family. But a quick run-through of this list will tell you quickly where the strengths and weaknesses of your preps are.

DECLUTTER AND GET ORGANIZED

Now is a good time to clean up and organize your home as you begin to take stock of what you have and make plans to acquire needed items and supplies. It will be much easier to complete the projects in later sections of this book as well if you get rid of the clutter of unwanted or no longer needed stuff.

ACTIVITY 1.3: **BASIC EMERGENCY SUPPLIES**

The following essential items should be in your home at all times.

BASIC EMERGENCY SUPPLIES

- ☐ Bottled drinking water
- ☐ Means of purifying contaminated water
- ☐ Foods that can be eaten without cooking
- ☐ Non-perishable foods (canned goods, rice, pasta, etc.)
- ☐ Non-electric can opener or multitool with opener
- ☐ Means of cooking without utilities (charcoal or propane grill, camp stove, etc.)
- ☐ Emergency blankets, sleeping bags, etc.
- ☐ Portable shelter (tarp or tent)
- ☐ Clothing: outer rain/wind/cold protection, insulating under layers
- ☐ Emergency heating (woodstove, propane stove, etc.)
- ☐ Flashlights, battery-powered lanterns
- ☐ Spare batteries
- ☐ Oil or kerosene lanterns, emergency candles

- ☐ Matches and/or butane lighters, FireSteel, etc.
- ☐ Pocket knife or multitool, larger cutting tool such as axe or machete
- ☐ Basic hand tools (hammer, screwdrivers, wrenches, saws, etc.)
- ☐ Solar or battery-powered cell phone charger
- ☐ Emergency weather radio (battery or hand-crank powered)
- ☐ Hand-held two-way communication radios (such as FRS radios)
- ☐ First aid supplies
- ☐ Hygiene supplies
- ☐ Protection (pepper spray, firearms, etc.)
- ☐ Emergency cash and/or rolled coins
- ☐ Reliable transportation if evacuation is necessary (car or other vehicle or at least a bicycle for each family member if living where automobiles are not an option)

ORGANIZING YOUR HOME

In this section you will get down to the details of your home itself, whether it's an apartment, condominium, single-family dwelling or something less conventional such as an RV or boat. The first worksheet provides account numbers and passwords related to the everyday management of your home. The reason you should record this here in your workbook is that your home may be damaged or destroyed or you may be injured or killed and other immediate family members may not have this information on hand.

ACTIVITY 1.3: HOME SWEET HOME

You may be understandably hesitant to fill out all the financial information in the following worksheet, but if you can keep it secure, this information can greatly reduce the worry and hassle for other family members if the one who normally pays the bills and manages bank accounts is unable to do so. Remember, the amount of detail, such as passwords, that you include is optional, but if you at least record the account numbers, other family members will have a place to start.

HOME INFORMATION

Home Insurance Information

Provider and phone number: _____

Name on account and account number: _____

Passwords (optional): _____

Home Mortgage or Rental Information

Bank or landlord and phone number: _____

Name on account and account number: _____

Passwords (optional): _____

UTILITY INFORMATION

Electric Company Information

Name and number to report outage: _____

Name on account and account number: _____

Passwords (optional): _____

Gas Company Information

Name and number to report leaks or damage: _____

Name on account and account number: _____

Passwords (optional): _____

Water and City Utilities Information

Name and phone number: _____

Name on account and account number: _____

Passwords (optional): _____

Additional Provider or Account

Name and phone number: _____

Name on account and account number: _____

Passwords (optional): _____

FINANCIAL INFORMATION

Bank Information (1)

Bank name and phone number: _____

Name on account: _____

Account number(s): _____

_____

Passwords or hints (optional): _____

Additional info: _____

Bank Information (2)

Bank name and phone number: _____

Name on account: _____

Account number(s): _____

_____

Passwords or hints (optional): _____

Additional info: _____

Credit/Debit Card Information (1)

Bank name/Card company: _____

Name on account: _____

Account number: _____

Card security code: _____ Expiration: _____

Passwords or hints (optional): _____

Additional info: _____

Credit/Debit Card Information (2)

Bank name/Card company: _____

Name on account: _____

Account number: _____

Card security code: _____ Expiration: _____

Passwords or hints (optional): _____

Additional info: _____

ACTIVITY 1.4: **MAPPING YOUR HOME**

You may know your home inside and out like the back of your hand, but your wife, husband, son, daughter or visiting friends or relatives may not. And it may be that they find themselves alone in the house in a time of emergency. On the grid on the opposing page, draw your basic home floor plan and include as many vital locations and reference points as you can. Add notes if necessary to make these critical locations clear.

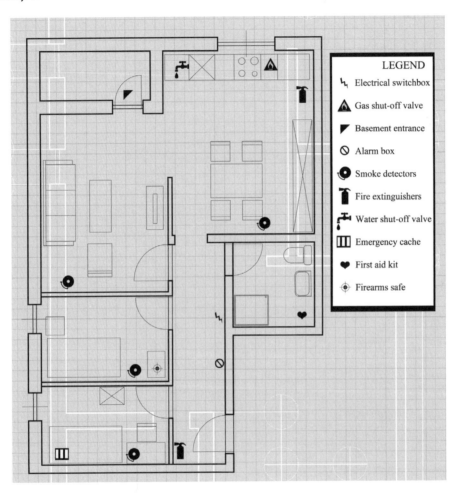

LEGEND

⌐ᴸ Electrical switchbox

🔺 Gas shut-off valve

◣ Basement entrance

⊘ Alarm box

● Smoke detectors

🧯 Fire extinguishers

🚰 Water shut-off valve

▮▮▮ Emergency cache

♥ First aid kit

⊕ Firearms safe

You should include a legend with symbols for the following items along with anything else you feel should be known:

- Electrical switchbox
- Gas shut-off valve
- Basement or attic entrance
- Alarm box
- Smoke/fire alarms
- Fire extinguishers
- Water shut-off valve
- Emergency cache
- First aid kit
- Firearms safe

HOME MAP

Notes:

_____

_____

_____

KNOWING YOUR SURROUNDINGS

The next step after you have organized and familiarized everyone in the family with the immediate dwelling, the accounts associated with it and the vital locations within it is to expand to the surrounding area to include the locations and contact information for emergency services and other nearby outside help. To do so, first complete the following worksheet with phone numbers and locations, then map these locations as explained in the next section.

ACTIVITY 1.5: VITAL LOCATIONS OUTSIDE YOUR HOME

Should an emergency occur, it is necessary to know where to go and who to call in order to get help, should help be available. List as many nearby emergency centers and services as possible:

VITAL LOCATIONS OUTSIDE YOUR HOME

Nearest Hospital: _____

Address: _____

Phone numbers: _____

Additional Area Hospitals: _____

Address: _____

Phone numbers: _____

Nearest Police Station: _____

Address: _____

Phone numbers: _____

County Sherriff's Department: _____

Address: _____

Phone numbers: _____

Nearest Fire House: _____

Address: _____

Phone numbers: _____

Nearest Vet or Animal Hospital: _____

Address: _____

Phone numbers: _____

Nearest Evacuation Center or Shelter: _____

Address: _____

Phone numbers: _____

Other: _____

Address: _____

Phone numbers: _____

ACTIVITY 1.6: **MAPPING YOUR NEARBY EMERGENCY LOCATIONS**

In this exercise, you will create a detailed and customized map that includes your home and its relation to the locations of the emergency service locations that you filled in when completing the previous worksheet. This should be a map that you can glue right into your workbook in the provided two-page spread so that you or any of your family members can find these vital locations at a glance. You can create this map from a standard street map from AAA or print it online from a site such as Google Maps. By adjusting the settings while printing or photocopying, you should be able to size it to fit the pages of this book. Once you have the map, mark the exact locations of the nearest hospital, police station, fire house, evacuation shelter, etc., as well as the best routes to reach them.

TIPS & TRICKS

GET COMFORTABLE OFF THE GRID

Just as family adventures can be a fun way to introduce everyone to prepping skills and gear, sleeping outdoors in a tent, traveling on foot or by bike or canoe, and doing without the conveniences of electricity or communications can give you and your family and edge in a disaster. If your children already know what it's like to go without modern technologies, their absence in the aftermath of a real event will not be such a shock.

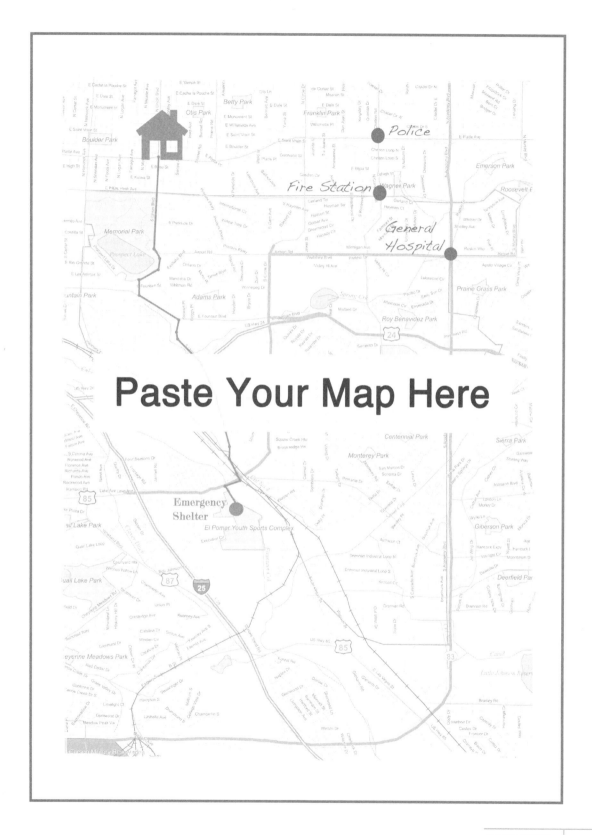

Paste Your Map Here

THE THREATS AROUND YOU

After assessing your home and mapping out its interior and its relationship to sources of possible help in the nearby community, it is now time to consider exactly what threats you may face and what types of emergencies or disasters you may have to contend with. One thing is certain: No matter where on Earth you live, there is no safe refuge from natural disasters or one kind or another, and with the current size of the human population on this planet, few locations are safe from manmade disasters either. You can, however, narrow down the kinds of catastrophes most likely to affect you by geographic region and factors such as your home's elevation above sea level and proximity to bodies of water, mountains, geological fault lines, etc., as well as human development such as cities and industrial complexes.

Historical weather data can tell you a lot about your location's vulnerability to storms such as tornadoes, hurricanes and blizzards, and can be researched on websites such as the National Weather Service and the National Hurricane Center. If you are new to an area, it would pay you to spend some time researching such historical data as well as news stories on more recent events. Talking to other area residents can enable you to gain valuable insight and tips as well. As you glean this information about specific threats to your location, go through the checklist that follows and check those threats that are known to or likely to affect you. Then, as you move forward through the rest of your workbook, you can tailor your preparedness plan to specifically deal with those threats, which will be outlined in detail later in this book.

TIPS & TRICKS

GET TO KNOW YOUR NEIGHBORS

Your immediate neighbors could have a significant impact on your family during or after a crisis. It pays to get to know who is living in the nearby vicinity and try and get an idea if they will also be self-sufficient and prepared. This could determine whether they might be helpful, indifferent or possibly even a threat when things go south.

ACTIVITY 1.7: HOW WELL DO YOU KNOW YOUR ZIP CODE?

The following is a checklist of common natural and manmade disasters that have caused catastrophic damage and loss of life where they occurred. Using historical data and current trends and information, go through this list and check all that may affect the area in which you make your home.

This is important: Make sure you do your research; don't just rely on experience. You may be shocked to learn that seventy years ago, an F4 tornado touched down half a mile from your home or that an active fault line runs along Main Street in your town.

- ☐ Tornadoes
- ☐ Severe thunderstorms (dangerous lightning and straight-line winds)
- ☐ Hurricanes and tropical storms
- ☐ Earthquakes
- ☐ Volcanic activity
- ☐ Tsunamis
- ☐ Flooding
- ☐ Winter storms and blizzards
- ☐ Avalanches

- ☐ Wildfires
- ☐ Industrial explosions
- ☐ Chemical spills or poisoning
- ☐ Pipeline or refinery accidents
- ☐ Hydroelectric or other dam failures
- ☐ Nuclear power plant accidents
- ☐ Plane crash or railroad accidents
- ☐ Terror attacks
- ☐ Riot or civil unrest
- ☐ Disease outbreaks or pandemics

Now that you've taken stock of your home and what you have on hand, compiled your family's vital information and assessed your surroundings and the possible threats you may face, it's time to take this information to the next two chapters. There, we will evaluate the pros and cons of sheltering in place or evacuating, and go through the worksheets and activities to prepare for both options.

TIPS & TRICKS

DON'T FORGET TO PLAN FOR YOUR PETS

Many pet owners consider their pets to be part of the family and will take their needs into consideration when stocking up for a crisis. Be aware though, that if you have to evacuate to a public shelter for any reason, pets may not be welcome. Have a plan for them whether you are sheltering in place or bugging out.

Chapter 2:
PREPARING TO SHELTER IN PLACE

THERE ARE ADVANTAGES TO STAYING PUT

To shelter in place, simply put, means that you (or the authorities) have deemed that you are safer where you are than if you were to attempt to relocate. It could be due to a pending or current threat or that an event has happened and officials must clear a nearby area of hazards. Sheltering in place offers the benefit of operating on your own turf. You know what you supplies you have available, what protection is at your disposal, and what needs you may have. Your familiarization with your surroundings is your greatest benefit. Beyond the basic needs, sheltering in place also offers psychological benefits that are vitally important as well. People are more calm, happy, and confident in familiar surroundings.

Sheltering in place can take on many forms. Since disasters can occur with little or no warning, you could be at home, work, the store, or even in your vehicle. So careful consideration must be given to whether to stay put or move on.

This flow chart can help you decide if sheltering in place is right for you.

FLOWCHART TO DETERMINE IF IT IS SAFE TO SHELTER IN PLACE

(Note: This flowchart cannot possibly contain every variable, but will help you assess the situation and make a logical decision.)

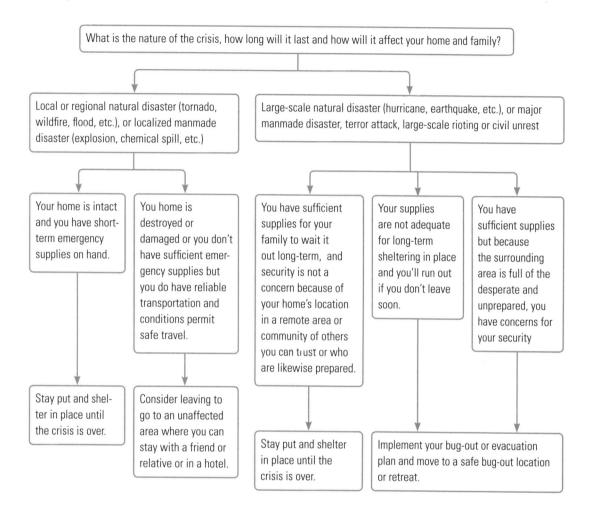

What is the nature of the crisis, how long will it last and how will it affect your home and family?

Local or regional natural disaster (tornado, wildfire, flood, etc.), or localized manmade disaster (explosion, chemical spill, etc.)

Large-scale natural disaster (hurricane, earthquake, etc.), or major manmade disaster, terror attack, large-scale rioting or civil unrest

Your home is intact and you have short-term emergency supplies on hand.

You home is destroyed or damaged or you don't have sufficient emergency supplies but you do have reliable transportation and conditions permit safe travel.

You have sufficient supplies for your family to wait it out long-term, and security is not a concern because of your home's location in a remote area or community of others you can trust or who are likewise prepared.

Your supplies are not adequate for long-term sheltering in place and you'll run out if you don't leave soon.

You have sufficient supplies but because the surrounding area is full of the desperate and unprepared, you have concerns for your security

Stay put and shelter in place until the crisis is over.

Consider leaving to go to an unaffected area where you can stay with a friend or relative or in a hotel.

Stay put and shelter in place until the crisis is over.

Implement your bug-out or evacuation plan and move to a safe bug-out location or retreat.

TIPS & TRICKS

YOU CAN EAT YOUR SOUP COLD

The food inside any canned good is perfectly safe to be eaten cold if you don't have a fire source. You can also safely heat up the canned food right in the can itself: Simply open the can, heat and eat.

BUILDING YOUR HOME'S EMERGENCY SUPPLIES

Many of the things necessary for survival are already in your home. But how many of those things rely on electricity, natural gas, or running water? When basic utilities are no longer available to you, many of the things that you use on a day-to-day basis no longer function or become obsolete. You will be forced to rely on your preparations.

The thought of all-encompassing readiness can by dizzying. Where do you begin? The good news is that it that the process can be as simple or as involved as you want it to be. Within the parameters of health and safety, the amount of preparation you may want to do is completely customizable. Supply your home with the supplies, food, and comforts that work for you!

Available space, what to put in that space and cost are the greatest concerns and considerations when beginning your preparations. Most people have neither the time nor money to have a fully operational survival bunker built in their backyard. In fact, many families are lucky to be able procure a corner in the basement or a shelf in a closet for preparation inventory. Identifying your available space will help you control how involved your preparation can become. Work within the area you are able to designate to store preparatory items. It is not uncommon to have multiple areas for storage. It depends on what is feasible for you.

FEMA recommends a minimum of 72 hours worth of preparations for you and your family. Use that as a starting point as you progress through the *The Prepper's Workbook*, customizing the build-your-own checklists found here to make them functional for you.

ACTIVITY 2.1: BUILDING YOUR EMERGENCY SUPPLY CHECKLISTS

This first list will help you ensure that you have the basic emergency supplies that should be in every home. Because no two families will need exactly the same list of items or supplies, this worksheet allows you to create your own list by adding suggested items from each of the different categories that follow. In building your list, be specific. For example, when you see a suggested item like "flashlights" in the category of ESSENTIAL ITEMS, write down the specific flashlights you have on hand or will buy for the purpose, along with the quantity: (AA-cell Mini-Maglights (2), 6-volt Coleman Lantern (1), and so on.) This way you will know exactly what you have on hand in your emergency supplies.

(Note: Stored food and drinking water are not included in this emergency supply list because there are separate build-your-own checklists that follow for those items.)

GENERAL ESSENTIAL ITEMS FOR SHELTERING IN PLACE

There are some essential items that you should have for any type of shelter in place disaster preparation. The "basics" are a great place to start as you begin your preparations, and there's a good chance you already have many of these items in your home.

GENERAL ESSENTIAL ITEMS CHECKLIST

❏ Generator and fuel	❏ _____
❏ Flashlights and batteries	❏ _____
❏ Portable radio/weather radio	❏ _____
❏ Matches	❏ _____
❏ Butane lighters	❏ _____
❏ Manual can opener	❏ _____
❏ Pet supplies	❏ _____
❏ Plastic sheeting or tarps for sealing leaks	❏ _____
❏ Area or city maps or atlas	❏ _____
❏ Eyeglasses/contact lens supplies	❏ _____
❏ Spare house and vehicle keys	❏ _____
❏ Medications	❏ _____
❏ Infant formula	❏ _____
❏ Diapers	❏ _____

PREPPER'S LIBRARY: VITAL REFERENCE MATERIALS

There is no substitute for knowledge and experience, but retaining the vast amount of information available in all areas of survival is a greater task than most are capable of. Keep a collection of essential titles nearby that you can quickly access.

FIRST AID AND SURVIVAL GUIDEBOOKS

- ☐ The U.S. Army Survival Guide
- ☐ The Prepper's Complete Book of Disaster Readiness
- ☐ Prepper's Long-Term Survival Guide
- ☐ Bug Out: The Complete Plan for Escaping a Catastrophic Disaster Before It's Too Late
- ☐ The Prepper's Pocket Guide
- ☐ How to Stay Alive in the Woods: A Complete Guide to Food, Shelter and Self-Preservation Anywhere
- ☐ Outdoor Survival Skills
- ☐ Mountaineering First Aid

- ☐ The Outward Bound Wilderness First-Aid Handbook
- ☐ Bushcraft: Outdoor Skills and Wilderness Survival
- ☐ Deep Survival: Who Lives, Who Dies and Why
- ☐ Survive!: Essential Skills to Get You Out of Anywhere Alive
- ☐ How to Survive the End of the World as We Know It: Tactics, Techniques and Technologies for Uncertain Times
- ☐ SAS Survival Handbook, Revised Edition: For Any Climate, in Any Situation

(See full list of recommended reading on page 188)

(See full list of recommended reading on page 188)

TIPS & TRICKS

LEARN WHAT BURNS

The top five natural tinders for creating a fire are:

- dead/dry leaves
- fibrous tree bark
- dead pine needles
- dead/dry grass
- weed tops

HOME AND PERSONAL DEFENSE ITEMS AND PREPARATIONS

Often during a disaster situation, there is a breakdown of social services. Law enforcement becomes overwhelmed and cannot meet the demands placed upon them. Unfortunately, whether for personal needs or opportunistic greed, theft and looting become common. Make sure you have what need to protect yourself, your family, supplies and property.

HOME DEFENSE CHECKLIST

- ☐ Safe
- ☐ Firearm(s) (see Chapter 11 for more information on suggested firearms)
- ☐ Ammunition
- ☐ Pepper spray
- ☐ High-intensity flashlight/spotlight
- ☐ Extra locks
- ☐ Dead bolts or barricade items
- ☐ Safe room
- ☐ Prepared escape exit

- ☐ _____
- ☐ _____
- ☐ _____
- ☐ _____
- ☐ _____
- ☐ _____
- ☐ _____
- ☐ _____
- ☐ _____
- ☐ _____

SAFETY ITEMS

No amount of disaster preparations would be complete without safety equipment. Personal safety is paramount, especially in a disaster situation, because receiving aid may not simply be a phone call away. There will be a need to be self-reliant. The safety items you will want to have will depend on your comfort level. The checklist below has recommendations to get you started. Customize the list to suit your own needs.

SAFETY ITEMS CHECKLIST

- ☐ Fire extinguishers
- ☐ First aid kit (you'll build this in Chapter 4)
- ☐ Knives
- ☐ Leather gloves
- ☐ Blankets or sleeping bags
- ☐ Sunscreen
- ☐ Hat
- ☐ Sturdy footwear

- ☐ _____
- ☐ _____
- ☐ _____
- ☐ _____
- ☐ _____
- ☐ _____
- ☐ _____
- ☐ _____

TOOLS

BASIC HAND TOOLS

Make sure you have hand-operated tools on hand. An electric screwdriver is going to become useless fast if there's no electricity for two weeks.

- ❏ Hammer
- ❏ Set of screwdrivers
- ❏ Pliers
- ❏ Set of wrenches and sockets
- ❏ Assorted nails
- ❏ Assorted screws
- ❏ Duct tape

- ❏ _____
- ❏ _____
- ❏ _____
- ❏ _____
- ❏ _____
- ❏ _____
- ❏ _____

ADDITIONAL TOOLS AND EQUIPMENT

- ❏ Shovel
- ❏ Axe
- ❏ Ladder
- ❏ Broom
- ❏ Bucket
- ❏ Mop
- ❏ Rope
- ❏ Cordage
- ❏ Empty sandbags

- ❏ _____
- ❏ _____
- ❏ _____
- ❏ _____
- ❏ _____
- ❏ _____
- ❏ _____
- ❏ _____
- ❏ _____

GRID-DOWN COOKING

The ability to cook without the benefit of electricity or gas can be tricky. You will need equal parts skill and equipment. What things do you have to cook and eat in a grid-down situation and what do you need?

GRID-DOWN COOKING CHECKLIST

☐ Fire-safe pots and pans	☐ _____
☐ Fire grate or grill	☐ _____
☐ Charcoal	☐ _____
☐ Camp stove	☐ _____
☐ Stove fuel	☐ _____
☐ Forks	☐ _____
☐ Spoons	☐ _____
☐ Knives	☐ _____
☐ Paper towels	☐ _____
☐ Paper plates	☐ _____
☐ Bowls	☐ _____
☐ Cups	☐ _____
☐ Aluminum foil	☐ _____
☐ Zip-top storage bags	☐ _____

SANITATION

An often-overlooked aspect of disaster preparation is sanitation. Quicker than you think, trash and human waste can accumulate, creating a breeding ground for bacteria and germs. It is important to be proactive in keeping your area sanitary, and you will need the supplies to do it.

LAUNDRY AND CLEANING

☐ Soap	☐ _____
☐ Bleach	☐ _____
☐ Bucket	☐ _____
☐ Scrub brushes	☐ _____
☐ Towels and rags	☐ _____
☐ Large plastic trash bags	☐ _____

SHOWERING AND BATHING

- ☐ Solar back-up shower
- ☐ Soap
- ☐ Shampoo

- ☐ _____
- ☐ _____
- ☐ _____

TOILETRIES

- ☐ Toothbrushes
- ☐ Toothpaste
- ☐ Toilet paper
- ☐ Deodorant
- ☐ Feminine hygiene products

- ☐ _____
- ☐ _____
- ☐ _____
- ☐ _____
- ☐ _____

ADDITIONAL PERSONAL ITEMS

- ☐ _____
- ☐ _____
- ☐ _____
- ☐ _____

- ☐ _____
- ☐ _____
- ☐ _____
- ☐ _____

KEEPING YOUR FAMILY FED

Without question, if you've given any thought to disaster preparation, food is listed as one of your top concerns, and rightfully so. The body can function for a relatively long time without food. But just because you can go without food does not mean that you should. If your nutritional needs are not met, you are susceptible to weakness, illness and the inability to perform common tasks or make critical decisions. Food storage is easily one of the highest priorities for survival but there are many things to consider, including nutritional value, quantity, shelf life and preparation, among others.

Let's begin with how much food to keep on hand. As mentioned before, FEMA recommends a minimum of 72 hours worth of food for each person in your household. What you need to do is to establish what that means to you. Are you comfortable with just 72 hours worth of food for you and your family? If not, what is your comfort level?

I am preparing food for _____ person/people.

I want to have food stores for _____ days / weeks / months.

Filling in the two blanks above will give you exactly what you need to know to start your food storage preparations. It starts with simply knowing how many people you plan to sustain during a disaster and for how long you plan to sustain yourself/them. Some say, as a safety factor, add one to the total number you are preparing for to ensure enough supplies.

The next step is to determine your typical food intake, and the best way to establish that is to track it. It would be easy to guess or assume what you may need or want for sustenance, but to accurately pre-plan you should know what your typical food intake is and plan accordingly. In an optimum situation, you would have a balance of vitamins, minerals, proteins and carbohydrates. In a survival-type situation, you will have to make do with what you have at your disposal. Therefore, planning now and planning accurately can be the difference between simply having food and being nutritionally prepared. The following activities will help you plan, store and prepare food for you and your family.

TIPS & TRICKS

BUILD A PREPPING GARDEN

You don't need a large amount of land to create an edible garden. Many vegetables, edible plants and spices can be grown in small containers such as 2-liter plastic bottles, guttering cut into manageable lengths, even old shoes—basically anything that can hold enough soil to support growth and allow for drainage holes to be put in it. Be creative!

DO NOT STORE WATER IN JUICE OR MILK JUGS

Milk protein and fruit sugars cannot be completely removed from their containers and provide an environment that supports bacterial growth.

ACTIVITY 2.2: **CALCULATING YOUR FAMILY'S FOOD NEEDS**

Using the form on the next page, document your family's total food intake every day for seven days, including condiments and seasoning. Have everyone be as detailed as possible, and include ingredients and quantities in each dish, like this:

Scott's Lunch

Monday: ham sandwich with lettuce, mayo, mustard and tomato, apple, crackers

Tuesday: bowl of turkey chili with Tabasco, mashed potatoes, iced tea

Wednesday: bowl of vegetable soup, added salt and pepper, crackers and cheese, root beer

This will help you identify the amount and type of food you and your family consume in a one-week period. From that list you can better calculate your family's needs for two weeks, one month, or even longer periods. If you're looking to buy bulk food, we also suggest using an online food-storage calculator like the ones available at www.family-survival-planning.com and www.areyouprepared.com.

DAILY FOOD INTAKE CHART

Breakfast	Mid-Morning Snack	Lunch	Mid-Afternoon Snack	Dinner	Dessert
MONDAY					
TUESDAY					
WEDNESDAY					
THURSDAY					

Breakfast	Mid-Morning Snack	Lunch	Mid-Afternoon Snack	Dinner	Dessert
FRIDAY					
SATURDAY					
SUNDAY					

Additional condiments and preferences (ketchup, sriracha, etc.):

_____

_____

_____

_____

WHAT KIND OF COOK ARE YOU?

If you like baking from scratch, direct your food preps toward grains, milk, eggs, legumes, seasonings, etc. If you want ease, you may prefer add-water items such as dehydrated and freeze-dried meals. "Heat and eat" foods are also an option in the form of MREs (Meal Ready to Eat). A combination of each of those options will provide variety and offer you the best defense against menu fatigue.

ACTIVITY 2.3: **BUILD A FAMILY FOOD STORAGE COOKBOOK**

Part of surviving happily is having meals that everyone likes to eat. Use this opportunity to build your own cookbook of foods that everyone in the family likes that can also be stored. On the following six pages, craft easy family-favorite recipes that can be made and enjoyed by anyone in your group. If you're looking for inspiration on what to make using food storage, we highly recommend picking up any of these tried-and-tested prepping cookbooks:

- *Meals in a Jar: Quick and Easy, Just-Add-Water, Homemade Recipes*
- *The Prepper's Cookbook: 300 Recipes to Turn Your Emergency Food into Nutritious, Delicious, Life-Saving Meals*
- *The Survivalist Cookbook: Recipes for Preppers*
- *A Man, a Can, a Plan: 50 Great Guy Meals Even You Can Make*
- *Cooking with Food Storage Made Easy*
- *Cookin' with Home Storage*
- *Cookin' with Beans and Rice*

Breakfast

Recipe:_____

Recipe:_____

Recipe:_____

Recipe:_____

Breakfast

Recipe:_____

Recipe:_____

Recipe:_____

Recipe:_____

Lunch

Recipe:_____

Recipe:_____

Recipe:_____

Recipe:_____

Lunch

Recipe:_____

Recipe:_____

Recipe:_____

Recipe:_____

Dinner

Recipe:_____

Recipe:_____

Recipe:_____

Recipe:_____

Dinner

Recipe:_____

Recipe:_____

Recipe:_____

Recipe:_____

ACTIVITY 2.4: **FOOD STORAGE CHECKLIST**

Using the breakfast, lunch, and dinner menus from the Food Storage Cookbook worksheets above and the Family Food Needs records from Activity 2.2 (page 44), build a food storage checklist with the items and quantities you will need to make those meals that will meet your family's needs for the amount of time for which you wish to be prepared. Following are some general popular food categories and specific item ideas. Feel free to add anything you would not want to do without if you couldn't run to the grocery store and get it. Your list should be customized to best suit you and your family. As with the emergency supplies list, be sure to note each item specifically described along with the quantities stored next to the item description.

PREPPER'S PANTRY INVENTORY CHECKLIST

Persons in my party: _____   Number of days supply: _____

Bulk Dried Foods and Staples

- ☐ Rice
- ☐ Beans (black, pinto, kidney, etc.)
- ☐ Pasta
- ☐ Oatmeal
- ☐ Cereals (granola, etc.)
- ☐ Granola bars, cereal bars, etc.
- ☐ Jerky
- ☐ Nuts (almonds, walnuts, cashews, etc.)
- ☐ Seeds (sunflower, pumpkin, etc.)
- ☐ Fruit (raisins, banana chips, apples, etc.)
- ☐ Peanut butter, almond butter
- ☐ Wax-encased hard cheese
- ☐ Vacuum-packed milk and/or almond milk
- ☐ Powdered milk
- ☐ Powdered eggs
- ☐ Protein powder
- ☐ Protein bars
- ☐ Cornmeal
- ☐ Flour
- ☐ Complete baking mixes (pancakes, cornbread, cakes, etc.)
- ☐ Complete meals (freeze-dried camping meals, MREs, etc.)
- ☐ Crackers, pretzels, etc.
- ☐ Rice cakes

- ☐ _____
- ☐ _____
- ☐ _____
- ☐ _____
- ☐ _____
- ☐ _____
- ☐ _____
- ☐ _____
- ☐ _____
- ☐ _____
- ☐ _____
- ☐ _____
- ☐ _____
- ☐ _____
- ☐ _____
- ☐ _____
- ☐ _____
- ☐ _____
- ☐ _____
- ☐ _____
- ☐ _____
- ☐ _____
- ☐ _____
- ☐ _____
- ☐ _____
- ☐ _____

PREPPER'S PANTRY INVENTORY CHECKLIST

Baking Supplies

- ☐ Yeast
- ☐ Baking soda/powder
- ☐ Vegetable oil
- ☐ Canola oil
- ☐ Olive oil
- ☐ Coconut oil
- ☐ Shortening
- ☐ Vanilla

- ☐ _____
- ☐ _____
- ☐ _____
- ☐ _____
- ☐ _____
- ☐ _____
- ☐ _____
- ☐ _____

Canned Foods

- ☐ Tuna
- ☐ Sardines, smoked herring, etc.
- ☐ Chicken
- ☐ Corned beef
- ☐ Spam
- ☐ Beans
- ☐ Vegetables
- ☐ Soups
- ☐ Sauces
- ☐ Chili
- ☐ Fruit
- ☐ Canned juice, other drinks

- ☐ _____
- ☐ _____
- ☐ _____
- ☐ _____
- ☐ _____
- ☐ _____
- ☐ _____
- ☐ _____
- ☐ _____
- ☐ _____
- ☐ _____
- ☐ _____

PREPPER'S PANTRY INVENTORY CHECKLIST

Spices and Condiments

- ☐ Salt
- ☐ Pepper
- ☐ Tony Chachere's or other seasoning blend
- ☐ Sugar
- ☐ Cinnamon
- ☐ Hot sauce (Tabasco, sriracha, etc.)
- ☐ Soy sauce
- ☐ Ketchup
- ☐ Mustard
- ☐ Mayonnaise
- ☐ Powdered garlic

- ☐ _____
- ☐ _____
- ☐ _____
- ☐ _____
- ☐ _____
- ☐ _____
- ☐ _____
- ☐ _____
- ☐ _____
- ☐ _____
- ☐ _____

Comfort Foods

- ☐ Coffee
- ☐ Powdered coffee creamer
- ☐ Tea
- ☐ Bottled juice and other drinks
- ☐ Chocolate
- ☐ Gatorade or other powdered drink mix
- ☐ Popcorn
- ☐ Snack cakes
- ☐ Cookies
- ☐ Hard candy
- ☐ Beer, liquor

- ☐ _____
- ☐ _____
- ☐ _____
- ☐ _____
- ☐ _____
- ☐ _____
- ☐ _____
- ☐ _____
- ☐ _____
- ☐ _____
- ☐ _____

KEEPING YOUR FAMILY HYDRATED (AND CLEAN)

Possibly the most important aspect of emergency preparedness is access to water. Clean drinking water is obviously important, but water is also critical for both cooking and cleaning. According to the Rule of Threes (survival is contingent upon you not exceeding: three minutes without breathing, three hours without shelter in an extreme environment, three days without water, three weeks without food), one only has a matter of days without water before dehydration can occur.

In both manmade and natural disasters, your home water supply may be cut off or rendered unsafe to drink due to contamination. Outside sources for usable water may be scarce or difficult to access. Therefore it is extremely important to secure and store sufficient drinking water for you and your family before the need arises.

ACTIVITY 2.5: CALCULATING YOUR FAMILY'S WATER NEEDS

To be on the safe side, it is a good idea to store at least 1 gallon of drinking water for each person per day (more for the very young, elderly, pregnant or sick, or those in hot climates). As with food, the minimum recommendation for home storage is three days worth of water per person, but again, you will likely want to increase the number of days substantially for any but the most minor disasters.

WATER STORAGE WORKSHEET

Total number of people in your family or group:_____

Number of days you are storing water for:_____

Minimum total = _____ people x _____ days x 1 gallon = _____ gallons total

Special needs = _____ people x _____ days x _____ gallons = _____ gallons total

_____ add totals above

Water Tips: The simplest way to achieve the required amount is to buy bottled water and keep the sealed bottles in a cool, dry place away from light and heat. Note the expiration date on the water and rotate every six months.

Keep in mind that an additional gallon per person per day should be stored for cooking and cleaning, though bottled or treated water isn't necessarily as important for such tasks.

ACTIVITY 2.6: **MAPPING YOUR HOME'S HIDDEN WATER SUPPLY**

On the following page, diagram your home and label the locations for your supplies of stored water. Remember there are alternate sources of water in your house other than the sealed, treated water that you have set aside for drinking.

Water Heater—The water heaters in most homes contain anywhere from 30 to 50 gallons of useable water. Water heaters are an often-forgotten supply of water that takes up no extra space in the home than it already occupies. Many people fail to even consider using the tank of water already in their home. Draining the water, though, should be a last resort because it is possible to damage the heating element by completely draining the tank. The challenge can be accessing the water for those who don't know how. Again, preparation is the key and you should learn how to drain your water heater before the disaster strikes.

1. Turn off electricity or gas to the heater.
2. Locate and close the water-supply valve to prevent water contamination
3. Locate the drain valve at the bottom of the water tank.
4. Attach a garden hose to the drain and open the valve.
5. In order for water to drain, air must be allowed in—open a kitchen or bathroom hot water faucet.

There is the possibility that the water is still very hot, and caution should be used when you're draining it. Also remember that hot water is drawn from the top of the tank, allowing sediment to settle at the bottom, which can obstruct the drain or make its way into your emergency drinking water. If you notice sediment in your water, simply allow it to sit for a period of time for the sediment to settle to the bottom of your container.

Toilet Tank—Typically the term "drinking water" is not used in the same sentence as "toilet." But in a critical situation, a toilet can be a perfectly viable source of usable water, unless your tank water has been chemically treated (example: blue water). Depending on the age of your commode, there is between 1.5 and 3.5 gallons of water in the tank that can be used for drinking, cleaning, sanitation or any other use. Water from the bowl should be considered contaminated and avoided.

Other Sources—If you take a moment to think about it, there are several other small water sources throughout your home. Some things to consider are the ice cubes melting in your powerless freezer and the static water in your household water lines; water can even be found in cans of fruits and vegetables. Unless otherwise contaminated, even swimming pool or hot tub water can be utilized for cleaning purposes.

Water Legend	
Potability	Symbol
Drinking water	
Cooking water	
Cleaning water	

SINGLE-SERVING PREPPING

After a trip to your favorite local fast food restaurant, you may end up with a few extra packets of ketchup, mustard, salsa, mayonnaise, honey, etc., in the bottom of the sack. Those are very handy to throw into a bag for conveniently packaged condiments in your preparation stash. Just remember to rotate based on their shelf life.

ACTIVITY 2.7: **LEARN TO PURIFY WATER THREE DIFFERENT WAYS**

Despite the fact that we live on a planet that is primarily covered by water, locating usable drinking water outside of a faucet or a plastic bottle can be surprisingly difficult, and if not done carefully, it can be dangerous. If you find yourself in a situation when you no longer have the luxury of drinking bottled water from your preparation supply because you ran out or failed to prepare at all, you may be required to procure water from an outside source. In that case, it is vital that you understand how to purify water. In this exercise you will familiarize yourself and your family members with three proven ways to purify questionable water: filtration, chemical treatment and boiling.

Filtering—Filtration is simply the process of removing many of the larger impurities in water. Water can be filtered by large, expensive filtration systems or as primitively as running water through a cloth or a cut-off plastic bottle filled with layers of cotton, charcoal and sand. But the best way to filter water is with a portable commercial filter designed for backpackers, wilderness campers and others who must purify available surface water for their drinking supply. Such filters are readily available from disaster preparedness suppliers and outdoor outfitters. Research the options and purchase one suitable for the number of people in your family. Then test it at a lake, river or other nearby source that is known to be free of chemical or industrial contamination, as no filter or other means can remove all such contaminates.

Chemical Treatment—Chemical water treatment can be as simple as adding a small amount of unscented chlorine bleach (about 8 drops to a gallon) to water, mixing well and waiting a half hour before use. Better options are commercial water purification tablets made for the purpose that will for the most part not affect the taste of the water. Iodine is another chemical treatment option, but unfortunately, on one of the best iodine water treatment solutions, Polar Pure, was recently banned by the U.S. government. Add some water purification tablets to your emergency supplies and take a 1-quart water bottle or canteen on a hiking trip or other excursion to test the treated water for taste. A big advantage of this method over filters is that purification tablets are small and take up little space. A disadvantage is that they do nothing to remove trash, leaves, sand and other solids from the water.

Boiling—The simplest and most common method to purify water is to boil it. A heat source and a container are the only requirements. Heat the water and bring it to a rapid boil. When it reaches its boiling point (212°F, 100°C), organisms and harmful bacteria are killed, allowing water to be safely consumed. The length of boil time is debatable. According to the Wilderness Medical Society, water temperatures above 185°F (85°C) will kill all bacteria within a few minutes. Since rarely in a survival situation will someone have a thermometer, bringing water to a boil is the easiest way to confirm that you have surpassed the appropriate temperature to kill bacteria. It must be noted that boiling water will not offer any safeguard against pesticides, herbicides and other hazardous chemicals that may contaminate the water. Because boiling water is such a reliable and safe means of water purification, a metal cooking pot that can withstand the flames of an open fire is highly recommended as part of your bug-out survival kit (see Chapter 3). For this exercise, take your emergency cooking pot and a means of starting a fire and see how long it takes from start to finish to purify water by boiling—including enough cool-down time to make it drinkable.

CARING FOR PETS BEFORE, DURING, AND AFTER A CATASTROPHE

For many, pets are just as much a part of the family as anyone and should be equally considered in all disaster preparations. You should be prepared to evacuate or shelter in place with your pet. Because most emergency shelters will not allow pets due to public health concerns, home preparations must be made or reservations at a pet-friendly location must be obtained early. You should also consider implementing a neighborhood "buddy" system to ensure care for each other's pets in the event of a catastrophe. In this section you will record vital information regarding your pet(s) and establish a checklist for caring for your pet before, during and after a catastrophe.

TIPS & TRICKS

HELP YOUR PET GET RESCUED

You can purchase pet evacuation stickers that, if your pet must be left behind, you can place on your front door to indicate what pets are in the home, how many and a phone number where you can be contacted if your pets must be/have been removed.

ACTIVITY 2.8: **PREPPING FOR YOUR PET**

PET VITAL INFORMATION

Pet name(s): _____

Pet breed(s): _____

Veterinarian: _____

Medical history: _____

_____

Medications: _____

_____

PASTE
PHOTO
HERE

Allergies: _____

Registration number(s): _____

Food (including brand): _____

Nearest animal shelter(s): _____

Nearest emergency veterinary care: _____

Pet-friendly evacuation location(s): _____

PET VITAL INFORMATION

Pet name(s): _____

Pet breed(s): _____

Veterinarian: _____

Medical history: _____

_____

Medications: _____

_____

PASTE
PHOTO
HERE

Allergies: _____

Registration number(s): _____

Food (including brand): _____

Nearest animal shelter(s): _____

Nearest emergency veterinary care: _____

Pet-friendly evacuation location(s): _____

PET VITAL INFORMATION

Pet name(s): _____

Pet breed(s): _____

Veterinarian: _____

Medical history: _____

_____

Medications: _____

_____

PASTE
PHOTO
HERE

Allergies: _____

Registration number(s): _____

Food (including brand): _____

Nearest animal shelter(s): _____

Nearest emergency veterinary care: _____

Pet-friendly evacuation location(s): _____

PET VITAL INFORMATION

Pet name(s): _____

Pet breed(s): _____

Veterinarian: _____

Medical history: _____

_____

Medications: _____

_____

PASTE
PHOTO
HERE

Allergies: _____

Registration number(s): _____

Food (including brand): _____

Nearest animal shelter(s): _____

Nearest emergency veterinary care: _____

Pet-friendly evacuation location(s): _____

PET PREPPING CHECKLIST

- ☐ Microchip and/or ID tag
- ☐ Medical records (sealed in plastic bag)
- ☐ Recent color photographs
- ☐ Collar
- ☐ Leashes
- ☐ Pet carrier/portable kennel
- ☐ Lightweight plastic tanks for fish or reptiles
- ☐ Food
- ☐ Water
- ☐ Food/water dishes
- ☐ Plastic bags for waste disposal
- ☐ Comfort items (blankets, chew bones, toys, etc.)
- ☐ Cleaning and hygiene supplies
- ☐ Pet first aid manual (like *The First Aid Companion for Cats and Dogs*)
- ☐ First aid kit for animals (optional)
- ☐ Written care instructions for your pet if it must be left behind

- ☐ _____
- ☐ _____
- ☐ _____
- ☐ _____
- ☐ _____
- ☐ _____
- ☐ _____
- ☐ _____
- ☐ _____
- ☐ _____
- ☐ _____
- ☐ _____
- ☐ _____
- ☐ _____
- ☐ _____
- ☐ _____
- ☐ _____
- ☐ _____

OTHER CONSIDERATIONS FOR SHELTERING IN PLACE

By this point you have most of your bases covered to shelter in place. You've considered stocking your home, storing food, purifying water and even taken care of your pets. This section will focus on the "extras." Sometimes it's the little things that make a big difference. Small comforts can go a long way in a disaster situation. They alleviate boredom and foster a more positive outlook that leads to better mental and physical health. Whether you are involved in a catastrophic event or simply snowed in for a few days without power, your overall experience could be vastly improved by a little bit of forethought to going beyond the basics.

Games and puzzles provide both a distraction and a mental workout. The devastation from the incident or the monotony of being locked in your own home can take its toll. Crossword puzzles, word finds or board games can take the burden off your mind, if only temporarily, and allow it to focus on a smaller, far less critical tasks. They keep your mind sharp and help to dull the edge of the event.

Also keep in mind small creature comforts. If money or space do not allow you to have a generator, consider a small solar charger that will allow you to power your mp3 player or cell phone. Make sure you have your familiar hygiene items such as a hairbrush or a favorite type of bath brush. Even without a catastrophic event, we all feel better once we are able to adequately clean and care for ourselves. Use this sample checklist to give you some ideas for your own "comfort" preparations.

ACTIVITY 2.9: STAYING COMFORTABLE—NON-ESSENTIAL ITEM CHECKLISTS

At this point you have covered most of your basic needs for disaster preparation. If you opt to shelter in place, one category that is easy to overlook is mental health. Studies have shown that the opportunity to groom and be entertained by things such as games and coloring books affords our brains a break from the disaster-related stress—a welcome and needed temporary diversion. Without the ability to use technology, we are forced to revert back to more basic forms of recreation. The following list is a good start. What comfort items will you want to have if you need to shelter in place?

ENTERTAINMENT FOR ADULTS

- [ ] Crosswords
- [ ] Sudokus
- [ ] Puzzle books
- [ ] Playing cards
- [ ] Books
- [ ] E-reader
- [ ] MP3 player
- [ ] Solar charger with USB port

- [ ] _____
- [ ] _____
- [ ] _____
- [ ] _____
- [ ] _____
- [ ] _____
- [ ] _____
- [ ] _____

ENTERTAINMENT FOR YOUNG KIDS

- [ ] Paper
- [ ] Pens
- [ ] Pencils
- [ ] Crayons
- [ ] Coloring books
- [ ] Board games
- [ ] Puzzle books
- [ ] Kids' books

- [ ] _____
- [ ] _____
- [ ] _____
- [ ] _____
- [ ] _____
- [ ] _____
- [ ] _____
- [ ] _____

COSMETIC

- [ ] Hairbrush
- [ ] Razor
- [ ] Cosmetics
- [ ] Nail clippers and other grooming tools
- [ ] Extra eyeglasses
- [ ] Contact supplies

- [ ] _____
- [ ] _____
- [ ] _____
- [ ] _____
- [ ] _____
- [ ] _____

MISCELLANEOUS

- ☐ Scented candles
- ☐ Hard candy
- ☐ Gum or other comfort foods
- ☐ Tobacco or alcohol products if desired

- ☐ _____
- ☐ _____
- ☐ _____
- ☐ _____

Sometimes a situation will dictate that the best action you can take is to stay put. If you've successfully stockpiled for a shelter-at-home scenario, and you've gone through each one of these checklists, you should feel very comfortable knowing that you have identified the things that you and your family will need to sustain a disaster in the relative "comfort" of your own home. There is a sense of accomplishment and confidence when you have done the work to sustain your family in the familiarity of your own house. This will serve you well as you move forward through *The Prepper's Workbook*.

Chapter 3:
PREPARING TO BUG OUT

THE BUG-OUT OR EVACUATION OPTION

Despite the many advantages to sheltering in place among your familiar surroundings and possessions, you may find yourself in a situation in which staying put is not an option. If your home was destroyed or severely damaged, or if the event is ongoing and there is a threat of more damage to it or danger to you and your family if you stay, then it makes little sense to hang around and it's time to Get Out of Dodge. Use the flowchart that follows to size up the situation and help you determine if it's better to stay or time to go. It's important to weigh all the factors when making this decision, because at some point, whether you stay or go, you will likely be committed and it will be too late to do anything about it if you made the wrong choice. Here are some potential scenarios in which evacuation could be the only viable option:

- Your home has been completely destroyed or rendered uninhabitable.

- You are certain your home will be destroyed or severely damaged.

- Staying at home puts you and your family in the path of a storm or disaster that could kill you if you remain in place.

- In the aftermath, your home is in the midst of large numbers of desperate people you cannot protect your family or supplies from.

- Generally, the more densely populated your home area is, the more likely it is you will have to leave. Relief and rescue services will be strained to the limit.

If you find that you do have to make the decision to bug out, knowing when and where to go and what to take with you will eliminate the unknowns, which are the major downsides to leaving your home turf. Remember, you will not be alone if you evacuate in the aftermath or during the threat of a major catastrophe, and you could be caught up in a gridlock with masses of panicked, much less prepared people. The remainder of this chapter will help you build a solid, viable bug-out plan that will take most of the unknowns out of the equation.

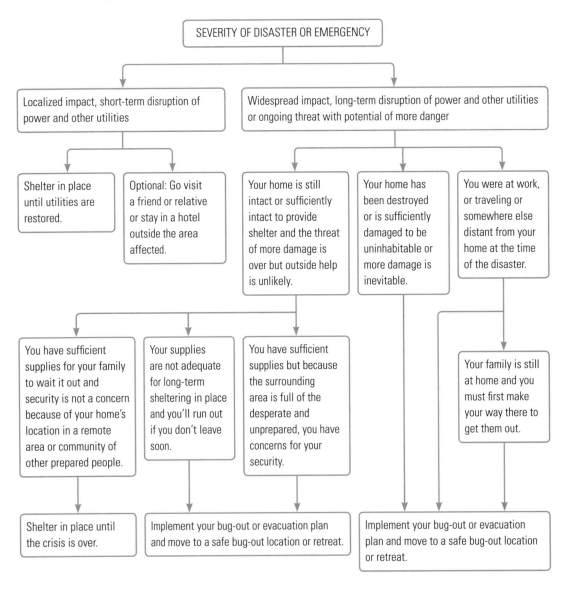

BUILDING A BUG-OUT BAG FOR THE HOME

The bug-out bag is simply a way to carry the things that you will need to survive while on the move and when you get to your destination. To some, the bug-out bag is a minimal 72-hour emergency kit designed to see you through the first three days of a disaster until you can reach an unaffected area or other safe haven. Some survivalists and preppers approach the bug-out bag from the other extreme, anticipating an ultimate doomsday scenario after which they will have to survive long term with the gear and supplies they have with them. You can tailor the contents of your own bug-out bag as you build your overall bug-out plan following the steps in this chapter, deciding what to take based on factors such as climate, season, distance you expect to have to travel and so on. The important thing about the bug-out bag is that it provides a central place to put all this gear in a package that you can quickly grab, strap on and move out with. The last thing you want to do in a situation that warrants bugging out is to have to dig through closets and drawers all over your house trying to round up the essentials. You should have one for every member of your family who is old enough or able to carry at least some of their own gear. In the checklist-building exercise that follows you will customize the contents of your bug-out bag(s) by adding the items that you need from each of the following major categories:

- The bag itself and the clothing you will be wearing when leaving
- Additional clothing for anticipated conditions
- Portable shelter, shelter-making tools and sleeping system
- Fire-making tools and materials
- Water supply and means of water purification
- Food supply and means to obtain and prepare more
- First aid kit
- Means of self-defense and family protection
- Miscellaneous

ACTIVITY 3.1: BUILDING A BUG-OUT BAG CHECKLIST

Since there is no one, all-inclusive bug-out bag checklist that is right for everyone in every situation, you will have to build your own, keeping in mind that you may end up changing it and adjusting the contents as seasons, conditions, technologies and your own experience levels change. The fill-in-the blank bug-out bag checklist pages that follow are broken down into the gear and supplies categories listed above. At the beginning of each checklist page is a generic list of items for that category. Again, not all will apply to your needs. Choose items you already have or purchase those you need to make sure you have adequately covered each category. When making your detailed lists, be specific and write down the exact name and if applicable, model number and quantity of the item. (Example: Columbia Goretex parka, Mountain Hardware sleeping bag, Leatherman Wave Multitool, Eureka Timberline tent, Bic butane lighters (10), Garmin 60cx GPS, Mountain House freeze-dried dinners (5), and so on.) This will ensure that you know exactly what is in your bug-out bag at all times, eliminating the need to waste time checking and re-checking specific items.

BUG-OUT BAG/BACKPACK

- ☐ Internal frame pack with load-distributing hip belt
- ☐ Smaller fanny pack or belt pack

☐ _____
☐ _____
☐ _____

Essential Clothing

- ☐ Belt
- ☐ Web gear
- ☐ Boots or shoes
- ☐ Socks
- ☐ Underwear/long underwear
- ☐ Pants
- ☐ Shorts
- ☐ Shirt
- ☐ Rainwear/poncho
- ☐ Cold-weather clothing
- ☐ Hat/balaclava
- ☐ Gloves/mittens

☐ _____
☐ _____
☐ _____
☐ _____
☐ _____
☐ _____
☐ _____
☐ _____
☐ _____
☐ _____
☐ _____
☐ _____

BUG-OUT BAG/BACKPACK

Additional Clothing for Anticipated Extreme Conditions

- ☐ Extra socks
- ☐ Spare shoes or river sandals
- ☐ Spare underwear/long underwear
- ☐ Bandanas
- ☐ Extra shirts
- ☐ Extra pants or shorts
- ☐ Fleece or other insulating layers
- ☐ Outwear depending on season and climate
- ☐ Rain gear
- ☐ Hats
- ☐ Camouflage clothing

☐ _____
☐ _____
☐ _____
☐ _____
☐ _____
☐ _____
☐ _____
☐ _____
☐ _____
☐ _____
☐ _____

Portable Shelter, Shelter-Making Tools and Sleeping System

- ☐ Tarp
- ☐ Tent
- ☐ Camping hammock
- ☐ Sleeping pad
- ☐ Sleeping bag
- ☐ Camp pillow
- ☐ Paracord or similar
- ☐ Tent stakes
- ☐ Axe, hatchet or machete

☐ _____
☐ _____
☐ _____
☐ _____
☐ _____
☐ _____
☐ _____
☐ _____
☐ _____

BUG-OUT BAG/BACKPACK

Fire-making Tools and Materials

☐ Waterproof matches

☐ Disposable butane lighters

☐ FireSteel or other alternative fire-starting tools

☐ Vaseline-soaked cotton balls

☐ Fire Sticks or other easily ignited tinder/kindling materials

Water Supply and Means of Water Purification

☐ Required amount of safe drinking water for amount of time anticipated ready to transport

☐ Extra water bottles, canteens or flexible bladder containers

☐ Water filter pumps

☐ Filter straws or osmosis filters

☐ Chemical water purification tablets or solutions (chlorine, iodine, etc.)

☐ Metal pot for boiling water in campfire flames

☐ _____

☐ _____

☐ _____

☐ _____

☐ _____

☐ _____

☐ _____

☐ _____

☐ _____

☐ _____

☐ _____

☐ _____

☐ _____

☐ _____

☐ _____

☐ _____

TIPS & TRICKS

YOUR RECREATIONAL VEHICLE OR BOAT CAN DOUBLE AS A BUG-OUT RETREAT

If you own a camper trailer, motorhome or cruising sailboat, powerboat or houseboat, you can customize and modify it to do double duty as a retreat shelter. Such a retreat can be either mobile to double as your bug-out transportation or kept in a separate, fixed location a safe distance from any disaster that may affect your home.

BUG-OUT BAG/BACKPACK

The following is your absolute bare minimum of food supply. It's meant to get you through the first week of survival, and the key here is to get bang for your buck—or rather calories for your pounds. Everything on this list is energy packed and fairly lightweight, exactly what you'll need if you're forced to be on the move.

Preliminary Food Supply

- ☐ 3-day supply of MREs, lifeboat rations or other meals requiring no cooking
- ☐ Trail mix
- ☐ Nuts
- ☐ Energy bars
- ☐ Dried fruit
- ☐ Jerky
- ☐ Peanut butter
- ☐ Granola
- ☐ Oatmeal
- ☐ Freeze-dried meals
- ☐ Quick rice
- ☐ Pasta
- ☐ Salt
- ☐ Alternative seasoning mix with salt and pepper blend

Cooking Utensils

- ☐ Spoon
- ☐ Cooking pot with lid (also used to purify water and included in water supply checklist on page 74)
- ☐ Aluminum foil

☐ _____
☐ _____
☐ _____
☐ _____
☐ _____
☐ _____
☐ _____
☐ _____
☐ _____
☐ _____
☐ _____
☐ _____
☐ _____
☐ _____
☐ _____
☐ _____

☐ _____
☐ _____
☐ _____
☐ _____
☐ _____

BUG-OUT BAG/BACKPACK

Hunting, Butchering and Survival Gear

- ☐ Fishhooks
- ☐ Monofilament line
- ☐ Trot line
- ☐ Small cast net
- ☐ Wire snares
- ☐ .22 or other preferred rifle or handgun, ammo
- ☐ Hunting knife, fillet knife

☐ _____
☐ _____
☐ _____
☐ _____
☐ _____
☐ _____
☐ _____

Bug-Out First Aid Kit and Supplies

- ☐ Adhesive bandages
- ☐ Gauze dressing
- ☐ Medical tape
- ☐ Duct tape
- ☐ Sterile gloves
- ☐ Antibiotic ointment
- ☐ Burn ointment
- ☐ Tweezers
- ☐ Pain reliever
- ☐ Benadryl
- ☐ Antidiarrheal medication
- ☐ Snake/insect bite kit
- ☐ Cortisone cream
- ☐ Eye drops
- ☐ Emergency dental kit

☐ _____
☐ _____
☐ _____
☐ _____
☐ _____
☐ _____
☐ _____
☐ _____
☐ _____
☐ _____
☐ _____
☐ _____
☐ _____
☐ _____
☐ _____

BUG-OUT BAG/BACKPACK

Means of Self-Defense and Family Protection

- ☐ (Rifle listed above)
- ☐ Spare magazines and ammo for rifle
  (_____ x _____rds. each, or _____rds.
  total if no magazines)
- ☐ Handgun
- ☐ Spare magazines and ammo for handgun
  (_____ x _____rds. each or _____rds.
  if revolver)
- ☐ Shotgun
- ☐ Shotgun shells _____rds.
- ☐ Firearms cleaning kit
- ☐ Pepper spray or mace
- ☐ Pepper spray for small animals
  (like dogs)
- ☐ Pepper spray for large animals
  (like bears)
- ☐ Folding or fixed-blade knife

☐ _____

☐ _____

☐ _____

☐ _____

☐ _____

☐ _____

☐ _____

☐ _____

☐ _____

☐ _____

☐ _____

☐ _____

☐ _____

☐ _____

☐ _____

TIPS & TRICKS

DUAL-USE ITEMS REQUIRE HALF THE WEIGHT AND SPACE

When packing you bug-out bag, try to consolidate as much as possible by choosing dual- or multiuse items. Many will be obvious, such as the ubiquitous Swiss Army knife or a firearm that can be used for both protection and procuring food. A good machete can take the place of a separate large knife, axe or hatchet, and camp saw. Use your creativity and find as many ways as possible to reduce the number of items you have to carry.

BUG-OUT BAG/BACKPACK

Miscellaneous Survival Gear

- ☐ Local area maps
- ☐ Compass
- ☐ Watch
- ☐ Handheld GPS
- ☐ Flashlight or headlamp
- ☐ Sunglasses
- ☐ Sunblock
- ☐ Insect repellent
- ☐ Knife sharpener
- ☐ Driver's license/passport/ID card
- ☐ Cash
- ☐ Optional: silver or gold coins for bartering

☐ _____
☐ _____
☐ _____
☐ _____
☐ _____
☐ _____
☐ _____
☐ _____
☐ _____
☐ _____
☐ _____
☐ _____

Toiletries

- ☐ Prescriptions (one month's worth)
- ☐ Small bottle of antibacterial soap
- ☐ Toothpaste
- ☐ Toothbrush
- ☐ Toilet paper
- ☐ Wet wipes

☐ _____
☐ _____
☐ _____
☐ _____
☐ _____
☐ _____

CONSIDER ALTERNATE TRANSPORTATION

In many areas, motor vehicles may not be the best option. A bicycle can get you out of a gridlocked city faster than sitting in a traffic jam with thousands of other cars. If there is navigable water such as a stream, river, lakeshore or coast, a boat may be the best option, as there will be far fewer people trying to leave by water routes, which are out of reach of those without boats.

BUILDING A BUG-OUT OR "GET-HOME" BAG FOR THE CAR/WORK

This checklist will help you build a smaller bug-out or "get home" bag for emergencies in which you might happen to be caught out somewhere in your car or at work. Unless you are traveling very far away, in most cases if this happens you will want to get back to your home first so you can make the decision to shelter in place with the rest of your family or implement you bug-out plan to Get Out of Dodge. For most people it may not be practical or affordable to have more than one complete bug-out bag such as the one you built in the previous worksheets, so you can cut down the contents of this smaller bag to the bare minimum essentials. Instead of planning for 72 hours or more, consider the time it might take to get home from your place of work or somewhere else you are likely to be stranded and pack just what you need for that time period.

GET-HOME BAG FOR THE CAR OR WORKPLACE

- ☐ Small backpack
- ☐ Walking shoes/boots
- ☐ Socks
- ☐ Rain/cold-weather wear
- ☐ Tarp or space blanket
- ☐ Knife or multitool
- ☐ Matches or butane lighters
- ☐ Flashlight/batteries
- ☐ Full water bottles
- ☐ High-energy snack foods (protein bars, etc.)
- ☐ Adhesive bandages

- ☐ Duct tape
- ☐ Pain reliever
- ☐ Benadryl
- ☐ 3 days of prescription medications
- ☐ Pepper spray or other simple defensive weapon
- ☐ Maps
- ☐ Compass
- ☐ Hand-held GPS
- ☐ Toilet paper or wet wipes
- ☐ Driver's license or ID
- ☐ $100 in small bills

ALUMINUM FOIL COOKING

Everyone knows that aluminum foil is great for cooking foods like potatoes, ears of corn or even steaks in the coals of a campfire. It can also be used to warm or cook the same kinds of food during a long evacuation drive by placing well-wrapped packages on the engine block of your car or truck. Just make sure to place in them in a location where they won't fall off as you drive.

EQUIPPING A BUG-OUT VEHICLE

Although there are many types of alternative bug-out vehicles such as ATVs, bicycles, self-contained RVs and even watercraft ranging from canoes to live-aboard cruisers, for most people the bug-out vehicle will be a car, SUV or pickup already in use for everyday transportation. If you already drive a rugged, four-wheel-drive SUV or truck with extra equipment, you may not need to do much of anything to make it ready. Other vehicles can be improved with some modifications, or if you're really concerned, you can trade what you have for something more suitable. Here are some desirable features and options that make a vehicle better for bugging out:

1. **Overall condition and up-to-date maintenance.** This is number one, because no matter what kind of vehicle you drive, dependability is the top priority. If your vehicle breaks down during an evacuation, you and your family could be put in a much worse situation than if you'd never left in the first place. Needless to say, you should carry a complete tool kit not only for keeping the vehicle running, but also the extras needed to clear obstacles from the road or dig out of the mud, etc. These will be considered in the checklist worksheet that follows.

2. **Ground clearance.** Good clearance between the road (or off-road) surface and the bottom of your vehicle's chassis and drive train will allow you to go over small obstacles such as curbs and debris without damage. SUVs and pickups are the best in this regard, while sports cars are the worst. The ground clearance of many vehicles can be improved by installing a lift kit or different suspension system.

3. **Four-wheel-drive or all-wheel-drive.** While you may not ever need it, having four-wheel-drive can get you out of a lot of situations and through obstacles like mud, sand, debris or water, up to a point. All-wheel-drive can also be beneficial for handling and safety in inclement weather, particularly rain, snow and ice. Do you need to trade your two-wheel-drive vehicle in for one with these options? That depends on your overall bug-out plan and includes factors such as where you live and where you plan to bug out to.

4. **Towing package.** A towing package with hitch and trailer light connections can greatly increase the utility of any vehicle for bugging out. Even sedans and all but the smallest of cars are rated for some towing capacity (check the manufacturer's labels) and towing a small utility trailer will allow you to take more gear and supplies, particularly if you have a large family that will occupy the interior. Trucks and SUVs can tow much more weight, and trailers with alternative and backup bug-out vehicles such as boats, motorcycles, ATVs and even horses are an option.

5. **Cargo racks.** Whether you plan to tow a trailer or not, cargo racks on the roof are a great addition to vehicles that do not have them as factory equipment. With them you can carry awkward loads such as canoes, kayaks and bicycles or building materials or extra gear. Cargo racks can either be permanently mounted or you can purchase quick-detachable systems that can be stored elsewhere when not needed.

TIPS & TRICKS

RESIST THE URGE TO GO BACK HOME TOO SOON

After a storm or other disaster is over, most people will have a powerful urge to get back home as soon as possible to check their property for damage. Resist this temptation until you know it is safe to return. Sometimes there is as much or more danger in the aftermath as there is during the height of the event.

ACTIVITY 3.2: BUILD A CHECKLIST FOR EQUIPPING YOUR BUG-OUT VEHICLE

This checklist will contain the tools and spare parts needed to keep your bug-out vehicle maintained and running and allow you to handle most foreseeable breakdowns on the road. It will also include items to help you free the vehicle if it becomes stuck or remove obstacles from your path, within reason. Like all of the checklists in this book, this bug-out vehicle checklist needs to be tailored to your specific needs, and your specific vehicle and its maintenance and reliability history.

BUG-OUT VEHICLE TOOLKIT, EQUIPMENT AND PARTS CHECKLIST

- ☐ Factory-supplied jack
- ☐ Hi-lift jack
- ☐ Tow strap
- ☐ Come-along
- ☐ Bumper-mounted winch(es)
- ☐ Lug wrench
- ☐ Extra spare wheel and tire
- ☐ Tire plug kit (Fix-A-Flat)
- ☐ 12-volt compressor or hand pump
- ☐ Air pressure gauge
- ☐ Metric or standard wrenches and socket set; depending on vehicle make, adjustable wrenches, channel-lock pliers, vise-grips
- ☐ Assorted flathead and Phillips screwdrivers
- ☐ Hammer
- ☐ Pry bar
- ☐ Spark plug wrench
- ☐ Jumper cables
- ☐ Multimeter
- ☐ Wire cutters/strippers
- ☐ Bolt cutters
- ☐ Shovel
- ☐ Tree limb saw
- ☐ Axe or chainsaw
- ☐ Engine oil
- ☐ Brake fluid
- ☐ Power-steering and transmission fluid
- ☐ Coolant/antifreeze
- ☐ Lubricating spray
- ☐ Duct tape
- ☐ Electrical tape
- ☐ Zip ties
- ☐ JB Weld glue
- ☐ Baling wire
- ☐ Assorted fasteners
- ☐ Spare ignition key
- ☐ Fuses
- ☐ Taillight and other bulbs
- ☐ Wiper blades
- ☐ Fuel filter
- ☐ Spare plugs
- ☐ Drive belts
- ☐ Alternator, starter, etc., depending on age and condition of existing

BUG-OUT RETREATS

The purpose of your own, personal bug-out retreat is to provide a place for you and your family to go in an evacuation so that you don't have to rely on public shelters or roughing it in a remote wilderness or other uninhabited area. Bug-out retreats require lots of forethought and pre-planning, as well as the expense and effort of setting them up. You may already own a vacation cabin or vacant land that is suitable for building a retreat, or you may want to start thinking about finding a place if you haven't. If you are committing your family bug-out plan to a fixed retreat, you will want to choose well, because in doing so you will have less flexibility once a disaster occurs and you have to use it. Here are some important considerations concerning bug-out retreats:

1. **Make sure you can reach your retreat when you need it.** Your bug-out retreat will do you little good if it is so far away or inaccessible that you can't get to it when you need it. In planning your retreat, you must consider your transportation options and make sure they are viable in the conditions in which you expect to need them.

2. **Your bug-out retreat won't be affected by the same disaster.** While it must be within reasonable reach if you need it, the retreat should also be far enough away and in different enough topography to be unaffected by most disasters that would cause you to flee your home. An example is a sheltered inland hurricane retreat a hundred miles or so from the coast—far enough to be safe from storm surge and the worst of the winds, but still close enough to get to. Another example is if you live in an area prone to flooding, make sure your bug-out retreat is on high ground.

3. **Remote, undeveloped or underdeveloped areas are safer.** Part of the danger of any evacuation is being swept up in the masses of desperate, unprepared people. Rural retreat locations offer more options, and when building your retreat shelter, you will come up against fewer restrictions and regulations than if trying to do the same in a town or city.

4. **Know your neighbors in the vicinity of the retreat.** Even in rural areas where you may have no immediate neighbors or even many in the vicinity, it pays to know who they are. It will do little good to evacuate your family to a retreat that has already been raided for supplies. If you trust your neighbors and they know your plans, they can be invaluable in looking out for your land and retreat while you are away.

5. **Is there a water supply? Are public utilities available?** Many suitable and affordable retreat properties may not have access to community water or utilities. If not, is it feasible to dig a well? Are you willing and able to set up a viable retreat completely off the grid? If so, it may be to your advantage, especially if the situation involves a widespread collapse of the grid anyway.

6. **Availability of natural resources.** What other natural resources are available? Is there surface water in the form of streams or ponds? Is firewood and timber available? What about the possibility of foraging for edible plants, or fishing or hunting for supplemental food? Again, the more rural or remote your bug-out retreat is, the more likely it is that you will have access to these kinds of resources.

TIPS & TRICKS

AVOID CONFRONTATIONS

Avoid confrontations at all costs. Many people you encounter may be desperate. No matter how well armed you are, you may be outnumbered or outgunned. Staying hidden, moving at night and choosing routes away from mass evacuation corridors are among the best tactics for avoiding confrontations.

WHERE TO BUG OUT TO IF YOU HAVE NO PERMANENT BUG-OUT RETREAT

Permanent bug-out retreats are not feasible for every family, due to home location, the cost of retreat property or other factors. There's no reason to despair if you don't own a retreat in the country somewhere. You may simply be able to go to a friend or relative's home, retreat or vacant land in an area not affected by the disaster. In smaller scale, shorter-duration events, checking in to a hotel or utilizing a public shelter may be an okay option. But every real bug-out plan will also include a list of nearby potential bug-out locations where you can survive unassisted for a period of time until the crisis is over. Such bug-out locations can be found on public lands or unused, remote corporate or private lands and other undeveloped areas. To narrow down your options, begin by studying detailed maps of your region, state and county, paying special attention to the following:

State and national parklands: Set aside for recreation and protection of special areas of scenic natural beauty or resources, these lands are for the most part uninhabited except for ranger stations and tourism-related facilities. After a major disaster they may be off most people's radar and could offer a place to shelter your family using the gear in your bug-out bag.

State and national forestlands: Like parklands, these are mostly uninhabited tracts of semi-wilderness that could provide a good place to hide out and set up a temporary shelter. Some will have resources such as wild edible plants, fish and game if you have the knowledge and tools to use them.

Other government-owned lands: The federal government owns millions of acres of land other than park and forest service lands. Look for Bureau of Land Management (BLM) and U.S. Army Corps of Engineers Lands in particular. Often these are vast tracts of uninhabited, remote lands in deserts, mountains and along rivers and other waterways. National Wildlife

Refuges are another option and are often good choices because they are managed for species habitat and protection, rather than human recreation. Depending on which state you live in, your state government may also own extensive wild lands within reach of your bug-out plan.

Private lands: You certainly have to be more careful when it comes to bugging out on private lands because of trespassing issues, but the fact remains that vast tracts of private lands are owned by absentee individuals or corporations based elsewhere. Sometimes, local knowledge of such holdings can be a great advantage because other refugees may be more likely to head for known parks and forestlands if they have no where else to go.

ACTIVITY 3.3: MAPPING YOUR PERSONAL ESCAPE ROUTES

Obtain local maps from AAA or pick up your official county or state road map and locate at least three potential safe bug-out locations within reasonable walking distance, biking distance and driving distance. Then mark or highlight each route using the above forms of transportation and glue the map onto the following page (folded is fine) so that you and all your family members can easily find it when you need it.

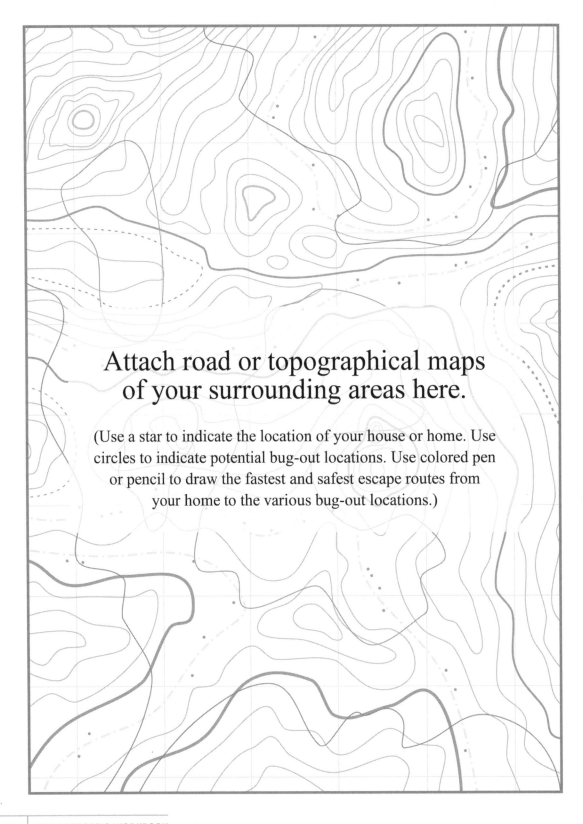

Attach road or topographical maps of your surrounding areas here.

(Use a star to indicate the location of your house or home. Use circles to indicate potential bug-out locations. Use colored pen or pencil to draw the fastest and safest escape routes from your home to the various bug-out locations.)

ACTIVITY 3.4: **WEEKEND ADVENTURE—MAKE YOUR WAY TO A BUG-OUT LOCATION BY FOOT AND RECORD IT**

This exercise gives you a chance to test your gear and planning by doing a trial run. In this case, you will be bugging out on foot, which is the most elemental and last-resort sort of scenario, but if you can pull this off, then adding a bike or any kind of motor vehicle in a real-life evacuation will be even easier. Use it as an opportunity not only to learn, but as an adventure the whole family can share. Keep a record of it here and use this information to fine-tune your plan or adapt a different strategy if needed.

Bug-out location destination and description: _____

Route taken (street names, etc.): _____

GPS coordinates (optional): _____

Travel time: _____

Estimated mileage: _____

Potential obstacles/dangers: _____

_____

_____

Gear/equipment overlooked or forgotten: _____

_____

_____

Gear/equipment taken but not needed: _____

_____

_____

Other notes: _____

_____

_____

_____

MAKING A FAMILY BUG-OUT/EVACUATION PLAN

In addition to the above steps to decide what you will take with you and where you will go if you have to leave your home, you will need to also consider contingencies such as the likelihood that not everyone will be at home when a disaster occurs. This level of planning includes:

Family discussions of possibilities: This includes going through all the "what-if" scenarios you can think of. What if you are at work or on the road when a disaster strikes? What if your wife is at work? What if your children are in school?

Emergency contacts outside immediate family: It's important to have phone number, e-mail address and physical address info for extended family members and friends outside the immediate area. Having such info for nearby neighbors is good too, in case you are away at the time of the disaster and need to find out the status of your neighborhood.

Alternative meet-up spots: These are pre-planned locations that everyone in the family knows how to find. It is a good idea to have such a meet-up spot in the nearby vicinity of your home, within walking distance, as well as a more distant one in case of a severe catastrophe. These meet-up spots could become critical to getting all your family members together if communications such as cell phones and landlines are disabled.

ACTIVITY 3.5: CRAFTING PERSONAL MEET-UP MAPS

Sketch or photocopy a small, wallet-sized map that includes the exact location of your preplanned meet-up spots. On the reverse side, include your emergency contacts and your family member contact info (from Activity 1.1, page 13). Under duress you may forget even your wife or husband's phone number if you are relying on memory, or like many people today, you may not know it by heart anyway.

Make one of these map/contact info cards for each member of your family and have it laminated for durability.

TIPS & TRICKS

CARRY A STAINLESS STEEL WATER BOTTLE

Instead of a plastic Nalgene water bottle or other canteen, consider carrying a stainless steel bottle instead, as it can be used to safely boil contaminated water and won't weigh much more. Although plastic bottles can be used to boil water in an emergency and it is a neat survival trick, doing so on a regular basis is dangerous, as the heat will inevitably leech toxic chemicals into the water from the plastic.

Chapter 4:
BASIC FIRST AID AND EMERGENCY RESPONSE

THE RULES OF BASIC FIRST AID

Whether there has been a catastrophic event or not, there are some skills that are beneficial to have regardless of the situation. The ability to perform first aid is one of them. Most people do not reach adulthood without having had to apply a bandage or two to a cut or wound. In some cases though, particularly a grid-down circumstance, having skills beyond simply applying a bandage are necessary. A little bit of knowledge and training can go a long way when the option to call for help is not available. It can be perhaps the most helpless feeling imaginable when someone is injured and you are relied upon to intervene. In those types of situations, being a spectator is not a likely option. The fears and anxieties that naturally occur can be diminished if you have taken first aid and CPR classes. Check with your local schools, churches and parks and recreation departments for classes available in your area.

Beyond the skill sets needed to perform first aid, you should be aware of the mental challenges. It is not unusual, in extreme scenarios, for people to feel fear, shock, sadness or physical and emotional trauma. Disaster victims can expect to experience any combination of these. Every day people are thrust into extraordinary circumstances when an event occurs and "the system" becomes overwhelmed, as do those affected. People are forced to revert to instinct and personal skill sets, such as first aid, to take care of themselves when the option to call 911 is not available. In this chapter we will discuss some first aid basics, create a family-specific first aid kit and highlight some first aid skills that everyone should know.

THREE RULES OF BASIC FIRST AID

There are some rules that are non-negotiable in any type of medical scenario:

1. The first thing that must be done is a "size-up." You need to determine the magnitude of the situation. How big or small of an event is it? What are the hazards? How many people are hurt and to what extent? You are in a gathering and processing mode, taking in a lot of information in a short amount of time in order to determine your best course of action.

   Establish a game plan, keeping in mind that personal safety is paramount. If you do not maintain as high a level of safety for yourself as possible, you become part of the problem rather than the solution. Also be aware of your level of comfort and training in handling medical emergencies. It is easy to become overwhelmed.

2. Don't panic. As long as the situation allows, this is the best time to take 30 seconds before you act. In most scenarios, half a minute will not affect the outcome and it allows you a moment of pause to develop your plan. The best remedy for situational anxiety is preparation. Knowing what to do and when do it negates much of the anxiety associated with a disaster.

3. When rendering medical aid, there are three times that you utilize Personal Protective Equipment (PPE): always, always and always. PPE should never be an afterthought. Something as a simple as eye protection and nitrile gloves provide a strong defense against bloodborne pathogens such as hepatitis and HIV. Nitrile is synthetic rubber that contains no latex. A common allergy to latex has forced medical professionals to evolve from their longtime use of latex to nitrile. Also, for your own safety as well as the victims', cover any open cuts or wounds that you have prior to rendering assistance to others.

ACTIVITY 4.1: WEEKEND PROJECT—CREATE A FAMILY-SPECIFIC FIRST AID KIT

Using the information you collected in Activity 1.1, put together a comprehensive first aid kit that includes wound care, prescriptions and any specific allergy medications, as well as treatment for any medical situations that may arise. If you have a personal or family doctor, often he or she can assist you with assembling this list. There are a variety of retail first aid kits available that can get you started with the basics, and you can build from that for your family-specific kit. Go through the folloing items to get some ideas, and then start your detailed list in the spaces that follow:

FAMILY FIRST AID KIT

- ☐ PPE (sterile gloves, safety glasses, medical mask, etc.)
- ☐ Alcohol-based hand sanitizer (at least 60% alcohol)
- ☐ First aid field guide (such as *The Survival Medicine Handbook*)
- ☐ 4x4-inch gauze
- ☐ 2x2-inch gauze
- ☐ Roll gauze
- ☐ Medical tape (one each of paper, plaster, micropore)
- ☐ Antibacterial ointment
- ☐ Variety-size package of adhesive bandages
- ☐ Butterfly bandages
- ☐ Super glue
- ☐ Normal saline
- ☐ Burn dressing
- ☐ Triangular bandages (with safety pins)
- ☐ Cotton swabs
- ☐ Ice packs
- ☐ Heat packs
- ☐ Trauma shears
- ☐ Tweezers
- ☐ Thermometer (with protective covers)
- ☐ Pain reliever (acetaminophen, ibuprofen, etc.)
- ☐ Aspirin
- ☐ Aloe vera gel
- ☐ Benadryl

- ☐ Insect bite treatment
- ☐ Antidiarrheal medication
- ☐ Antacid
- ☐ Prescription medication
- ☐ Activated charcoal
- ☐ Petroleum jelly
- ☐ Cold/flu medication
- ☐ Eyedrops
- ☐ Snake bite kit
- ☐ Emergency dental kit
- ☐ _____
- ☐ _____
- ☐ _____
- ☐ _____
- ☐ _____
- ☐ _____
- ☐ _____
- ☐ _____
- ☐ _____
- ☐ _____
- ☐ _____
- ☐ _____
- ☐ _____
- ☐ _____
- ☐ _____
- ☐ _____
- ☐ _____

QUICK GUIDE TO PAIN RELIEVERS

Your preparations would not be complete without over-the-counter pain relievers. We all experience pain in one form or another and have a variety of options to manage it. Consideration should be given to the different types as well as their purpose.

Aspirin was once a favorite pain reliever in the United States but has lost popularity due to its propensity to be harsh on the stomach, as well as its association with Reye's syndrome. Many adults still take it for pain management and it is often taken as a blood thinner but should only be taken as such under direction from a doctor.

Ibuprofen is a good all-around over-the-counter pain-management medication. It offers pain relief, fever reduction, helps alleviate cramps and decreases inflammation. It is sort of a pain relief catchall. Note that ibuprofen can cause irritation to the lining of the stomach so it should be taken with caution, as directed, and avoided if you have ulcers.

Acetaminophen is a popular over-the-counter pain reliever and is a common and effective fever reducer. It is actually a frequent ingredient in a variety of other medications. Acetaminophen can be safe for pregnant women and is even used to treat mild general anxiety. It can be taken in conjunction with ibuprofen to relieve a variety of ailments. Follow the recommendations because acetaminophen can be toxic in high doses. Also know that acetaminophen will not reduce swelling.

The same information applies to children, but the liquid forms are often used because it makes it easier for them to consume. Consult with your doctor about which pain relievers are right for you, which to keep in your disaster preparation supplies and why.

ACTIVITY 4.2: **FAMILY MEDICAL HISTORY**

Use the following space to record each family member's basic need-to-know information.

Name: _____

Date of birth: _____ Weight: _____

Blood type: _____

Medications: _____

_____

Allergies: _____

_____

Medical notes (previous ailments, medical history): _____

_____

_____

_____

Name: _____

Date of birth: _____ Weight: _____

Blood type: _____

Medications: _____

_____

Allergies: _____

_____

Medical notes (previous ailments, medical history): _____

_____

_____

_____

Name: _____

Date of birth: _____ Weight: _____

Blood type: _____

Medications: _____

_____

Allergies: _____

_____

Medical notes (previous ailments, medical history): _____

_____

_____

_____

Name: _____

Date of birth: _____ Weight: _____

Blood type: _____

Medications: _____

_____

Allergies: _____

_____

Medical notes (previous ailments, medical history): _____

_____

_____

_____

Name: _____

Date of birth: _____ Weight: _____

Blood type: _____

Medications: _____

_____

Allergies: _____

_____

Medical notes (previous ailments, medical history): _____

_____

_____

_____

Name: _____

Date of birth: _____ Weight: _____

Blood type: _____

Medications: _____

_____

Allergies: _____

_____

Medical notes (previous ailments, medical history): _____

_____

_____

_____

ACTIVITY 4.3: LEARN TEN EMERGENCY RESPONSE SKILLS EVERYONE SHOULD KNOW

1. Identify the ABCs

When you render first aid to someone, the first and the easiest things to evaluate are also the most critical: Airway, Breathing, and Circulation (the ABCs). This is typically done by simply asking something like, "Are you hurt?" If they are able to respond in any way, they have control of their airway, they are breathing, and their heart is beating. If they do not respond, intervention may be required in the form of cardiopulmonary resuscitation (CPR) or rescue breathing. They are always treated in order, first—airway, second—breathing, followed by circulation.

Tip: If someone appears to be not breathing, a simple "head tilt/chin lift" can possibly open the airway enough to restore breathing. The head tilt/chin lift maneuver is a basic procedure used in cardiopulmonary resuscitation to open the patient's airway. One hand tilts the head back while other hand is placed under the chin to lift the jaw and displace the tongue.

2. Learn How to Perform Wound Care/Bleeding Control

After donning the appropriate PPE, the first and most effective method to control bleeding is to apply direct pressure and elevate. Apply a sterile dressing (any gauze or cloth applied to a wound is called a dressing) directly over the wound and hold pressure. A sterile dressing may not always be available, especially in a disaster situation. Remember, any dressing is better than none. By holding and maintaining pressure, you allow the blood to clot. As long as there is no fracture, elevate the wound above the heart, to help reduce the amount of blood going to the wound. If you hold your hand up in the air for more than a few minutes your fingers begin to tingle. This is because the heart is having trouble circulating the adequate amount of blood that high; it is fighting gravity. Use gravity to your advantage. Direct pressure and elevation will control the majority of soft tissue injuries.

Tip: The application of direct pressure to a wound is something the patient can possibly do for themselves, allowing you to care for others.

3. Learn When and How to Apply a Tourniquet

A tourniquet is a tight band used to restrict or stop arterial blood flow. They have had a bad name in the field of emergency medicine for a long time but are coming back into favor in cases of extreme blood loss. There are many complications that come along with using a tourniquet including tissue damage and possible unnecessary amputations. Therefore, they should be used only as a last resort.

To apply a tourniquet:

1. Use a piece of cloth or elastic band, preferably 1 to 2 inches wide.
2. Place it 2 to 4 inches away from the wound toward the core of your body.

3. Use padding underneath the tourniquet to avoid cutting into the skin.

4. Tie a half knot (the same knot used as the first part of tying your shoe).

5. Place a stick (or similar rigid object) on top of the half knot.

6. Tie a full knot over the stick.

7. Twist the stick until the tourniquet is tight around the limb and the bleeding has stopped. Blood may ooze for a short time, and this is to be expected.

8. Fasten the tourniquet to the injured limb in a way that prevents it from loosening.

Warning: Only in the direst of circumstances should a tourniquet be considered. Applying direct pressure and locating pressure points are the best options. They are the easiest to perform and provide the least chance for complications.

4. Learn How to Recognize and Treat Shock

The term "shock" can refer to wide range of medical conditions. It means and looks like different things to different people. One important thing to keep in mind is that "shock" is not an actual diagnosis. It is a symptom of a bigger problem that requires medical attention as soon as possible. Shock can be caused by many different things, such as an allergic reaction, blood loss or severe infection. Basically, shock is when, for whatever reason, blood flow or blood volume is not sufficient to meet the needs of the body.

Shock Recognition:

Early Stages
- Cool/sweaty skin
- Rapid pulse
- Anxiety

Late Stages
- Weakness/dizziness
- Nausea/vomiting
- Rapid/shallow breathing
- Confusion
- Thirst
- Weakening pulse
- Cyanosis (blue around the lips and fingers)
- Loss of consciousness

Shock Treatment:

- Lie the victim supine (on their back)
- Ensure their ABCs (page 96)
- Control bleeding if necessary
- Elevate the feet 6 to 12 inches
- Loosen clothing
- Provide cooling or warmth to make the victim comfortable
- Seek professional medical care as soon as possible

Tip: The key to treating shock is early recognition. Once you recognize the signs and symptoms and understand that there is a bigger issue, you can begin to treat the victim.

5. How to Recognize and Treat a Concussion

The term "concussion" refers to a traumatic injury to the brain. Concussions are usually caused by a blow to the head, but can be the result of any of a number of causes such as being violently shaken or the concussion from an explosion. By definition, concussions are not life threatening and are fairly common, especially in contact sports. A typical concussion heals and is treated with very little, if any, intervention.

Concussion Recognition:

- Mental effects (difficulty thinking, remembering, or concentrating)
- Physical effects (headache, nausea, blurred vision, sensitivity to light, dizziness)
- Sleeping more or less than usual
- Irritability
- Anxiety
- Atypically emotional

Concussion Treatment:

Treating a concussion is basically managing the pain, rest, and reevaluation. Encourage the victim to stop physical activity, apply an ice pack if desired for comfort and offer over-the-counter pain medication. Continually monitor them for any changes in conditions. Seek advanced medical care as soon as possible to adequately determine the extent of the concussion and what, if any, further treatment is necessary.

A common "treatment" for concussion is to prevent the person from falling asleep. Many have heard or have even said themselves to keep the person awake following a head injury, but few know why. There is nothing detrimental that is caused by sleep. Sleep simply prevents you from recognizing signs such as an altered mental status or a loss of coordination, or prevents the victim from feeling symptoms such as a headache or nausea. Keeping someone awake after a suspected concussion is a good idea for a period of time to allow you to monitor them, but rest for the person should be mandatory.

Tip: Concussions, or mild traumatic brain injuries (MTBI), have a mortality rate of almost zero, and fewer than 1 percent require surgery. Mental and physical rest is the best medicine.

6. Learn How to Treat a Burn

Burns are caused by heat, chemicals, electricity, friction and radiation, and they are divided into three categories. The degree of the burn is determined by the depth of the damage to the skin. The skin is the body's greatest defense against infection. Burns damage and compromise the skin, which can lead to not only infection but dehydration and possibly even hypothermia. The main goals for treating a burn are to stop the burning process, prevent shock, prevent infection and ease pain. By determining the degree of the burn, you can determine the type of care needed.

First-degree burns are superficial and typically cause redness and pain to the outer layer of skin (epidermis). They usually heal with minimal treatment.

First-Degree Burn Recognition:
- Redness of the skin
- Swelling
- Pain

First-Degree Burn Treatment:
- Cool the burned area with running water or a cold compress.
- Apply topical burn ointment.
- Cover and protect the burned area with a sterile gauze bandage.
- Take over-the-counter pain medication.

Second-degree burns are slightly deeper into the second layer of skin (dermis) and cause significant pain and blistering. They may require advanced medical care if and when it becomes available.

Second-Degree Burn Recognition:
- Skin is a deep red and splotchy
- Significant pain and swelling
- Blisters typically develop

Second-Degree Burn Treatment:

- If the burn is small (less than 3 inches in diameter) and not located on the face, groin, hands, feet or on a major joint, treat as a first-degree burn.

- If the burn covers a large surface area or is located on one of the above mentioned critical areas, treat as a third-degree burn.

Third-degree burns (also referred to as full-thickness burns) are the most serious burns, causing damage to the subcutaneous layers of skin and pose a significant health risk. Receiving advanced care can be critical in the case of a third-degree burn. The skin can be black and charred or possibly dry and white.

Third-Degree Burn Recognition:

- Dry and leathery skin

- Skin may be black, white, brown or yellow

- Swelling

- Pain may be absent due to the nerve endings being destroyed

Third-Degree Burn Treatment:

- Clean the wound with sterile water and remove loose debris.

- Treat for shock.

- Do not remove burned clothing stuck to the wound.

- Cover the wound with loose sterile cloth.

- If possible, elevate the wound.

- If burns are to the face, check for breathing complications.

- DO NOT apply ointment, cream, ice, fluffy wound dressing, or medications to the wound.

Warning: Avoid household burn remedies such as applying butter, pouring alcohol or milk on the burn, and placing cold meat on the wound. Only use medical ointments or aloe vera.

7. How to Recognize and Treat Cold and Heat Emergencies

Cold Emergencies: Unexpected weather changes often lead to unexpected challenges. Cold weather, specifically, presents its own Pandora's box of problems, namely as it relates to the human body. A common misconception is that cold weather medical issues arise in the depths of winter or in heavy snow conditions. But the reality is that you can get into cold-temperature related difficulties when the sun is shining and there is not a snowflake to be seen.

The cold becomes problematic when the body's core temperature drops below the normal 98.6°F. If it continues to drop, the body is at risk of hypothermia. Hypothermia occurs when the body's temperature continues to drop below what it requires for normal function, which by definition, is 95°F. Keep in mind that the very young and the elderly are more susceptible to changes in temperature, and special care should be given to maintain a consistent normal body temperature.

Cold Emergency Treatment:

- First and foremost, move the victim into a warm environment.

- If the victim's clothes are wet, remove them.

- Begin active rewarming by placing the victim under loose, dry layers and by rubbing the skin.

- Drink warm beverages. Alcohol should be avoided. It is counterproductive to the body's natural processes. Alcohol increases blood flow to the skin, giving the person the feeling of warmth, when in actuality the body's core temperature could be continuing to decrease.

- If frostbite is suspected (grayish or white waxy skin and numbness), protect the affected area, but do not rub the skin. Body heat can be used to passively warm the affected area. The warmest areas of the body are the groin and the armpits. Actively warming the body, for example by laying the victim next to a campfire, is dangerous because the skin is numb and is at risk of burning.

- If hypothermia is suspected (shivering, confusion, memory loss), do not immerse the victim in warm water; it can cause heart arrhythmia. Instead, warm the person with layers of warm dry blankets and, if possible, use the body heat of another person.

Heat Emergencies: Disasters rarely happen in perfect weather. In fact, the imperfect weather is often the cause of the problems. All four seasons have their own inherent weather-related dangers. Heat emergencies are mostly attributed to summer, but spring and fall are not free from the threats of heat. Exposure to elevated temperatures and sunlight places people at risk, and unless skin protection and hydration issues are addressed, the body cannot function normally and it's ability to regulate temperature becomes compromised.

There are three main heat related issues: heat cramps, heat exhaustion and heat stroke. Heat cramps and heat exhaustion are mild heat-related illnesses that are easily treatable. Heat stroke is a later-stage illness that is far more serious. Early recognition of the signs and symptoms are extremely important.

TIPS & TRICKS

THE DIFFERENCE BETWEEN "SIGNS" AND "SYMPTOMS"

Signs are something that can be seen by a third party (sweating, bleeding, bruising, etc.).

Symptoms are felt by the victim (chest pain, headache, nausea, etc.).

Signs and Symptoms of Heat Cramps:

- Sweating

- Muscular spasms or pain, typically in the abdomen, arms or legs

Heat Cramps Treatment:

- Stop all activity and sit quietly in a cool place.

- Drink clear juice or a sports beverage.

- Do not return to strenuous activity for a few hours after the cramps subside because further exertion may lead to heat exhaustion or heat stroke.

- Seek medical attention for heat cramps if they do not subside in one hour.

Signs and Symptoms of Heat Exhaustion:

- Heavy sweating

- Paleness

- Muscle cramps

- Tiredness

- Weakness

- Dizziness

- Headache

- Nausea or vomiting

- Fainting

Heat Exhaustion Treatment:

- Drink cool, nonalcoholic beverages.

- Rest.

- Take a cool shower, bath or sponge bath.

- Seek an air-conditioned environment.

- Wear lightweight clothing.

Signs and Symptoms of Heat Stroke:

- An extremely high body temperature (above 103°F)

- Red, hot and dry skin (no sweating)

- Rapid, strong pulse

- Throbbing headache

- Dizziness
- Nausea
- Confusion
- Unconsciousness

Heat Stroke Treatment:
- Get the victim to a shady area.
- Cool the victim rapidly, using whatever methods you can. For example, immerse the victim in a tub of cool water; place the person in a cool shower; spray the victim with cool water from a garden hose; sponge the person with cool water; or if the humidity is low, wrap the victim in a cool, wet sheet and fan him or her vigorously.
- Monitor body temperature and continue cooling efforts until the body temperature drops to 101 to 102°F.
- If emergency medical personnel are delayed, call the hospital emergency room for further instructions.
- Do not give the victim alcohol to drink. Room-temperature fluids are recommended such as tap water or bottled water that has not been refrigerated.
- Get medical assistance as soon as possible.

8. Become Certified in Cardiopulmonary Resuscitation (CPR)

CPR allows you to assist an unresponsive person in cardiac arrest by keeping oxygen moving to their brain until help arrives or the person recovers. You are manually performing critical bodily functions for someone whose body, for whatever reason, isn't doing it for them. There are many businesses and organizations that offer CPR certification classes. The American Heart Association even offers a free 60-second online video to teach you "hands only" CPR. Sign up, get certified and be able perform crucial life-saving measures if the need should arise. Also note that every few years the steps of CPR are altered as statistics and science dictate. If you are certified and it has been a while, you should take a refresher course.

Tip: It may come as a surprise, but in a mass-casualty incident, CPR is typically not utilized. Unfortunately there is just not enough time for it. The goal is to do the greatest amount of good for the greatest number of people and CPR is labor-intensive and a statistical long shot. If time and resources allow, CPR should be performed.

9. Recognize and Treat a Seizure

A seizure occurs when the electrical activity of the brain becomes altered. These abnormal signals from the brain cause the body to convulse or seize. The cause can vary from person to person. Someone can be prone to seizures due to a seizure disorder such as epilepsy; seizures can occur when the body's core temperature quickly elevates; low blood sugar can cause a seizure;

or a variety of other reasons. During a seizure the body will shake (either violently or mildly) for a short period of time, usually a minute or two. Then the person will go into a "postictal state" where they can appear to be asleep or will stare off into space.

To treat a seizure, the best thing that you can do is to keep the person from hurting themselves and allow it to happen. Lay the person down, loosen any clothing around their neck and clear objects away that may injure the person having the seizure. Call 911 if it is available. Once the person has finished seizing, roll them onto their side in the "recovery position" to help maintain an open airway.

Tip: Do not attempt to stop the person from shaking. You won't. Also, do not insert any objects in the person's mouth. It can cause injury to you, the victim, or both.

10. How to Identify and Treat an Allergic Reaction

An allergic reaction occurs when the body identifies something as a threat. It begins to fight the substance (which is many times harmless—medication, pollen, dust mites, food, etc.). The body's reaction can result in minor issues (rash, itchy eyes, runny nose) or a more severe reaction (difficulty breathing or nausea). There are many types of allergies: seasonal, food, medicinal, animals, latex, etc. Allergic reactions are not necessarily a medical emergency. A severe reaction, called anaphylaxis, IS.

If an anaphylactic reaction occurs, call 911 immediately (if possible). There is no way to predict how severe the reaction will become and advanced medical care is needed. Many times people with a known severe allergy will carry epinephrine or an "EpiPen." An EpiPen is a self administered, measured-dose medication that can be injected in the case of an anaphylactic reaction. That person should be familiar with it and can usually tell you how to administer it.

Warning: DO NOT administer an EpiPen to anyone but the person to whom it is prescribed. Prescriptions can vary from person to person, and it is not safe to use someone else's medication.

PREPPER'S TOP TEN ESSENTIAL SURVIVAL SKILLS

The "top ten" list presented here outlines the essential survival skills that everyone interested in preparedness should strive to learn. They are not listed in any particular order, as we feel that all of them are equally important. None of these skills can be learned from reading alone, but instead require study, practice and in many cases instruction from others who have mastered and are able to teach them. The concepts and fundamentals of most of these skills are described in many of the books listed in the Recommended Reading section at the back of this book, and reading is a good place to start, but you will have to follow up by doing. Some of these skills, like navigation, hunting, hand-to-hand fighting and the use of firearms are pursuits that you could spend a lifetime perfecting, but whether or not you take it to extremes, you should at least strive to attain at least a basic competence.

1. LEARN TO LOCATE AND PURIFY WATER

Having an adequate supply of safe drinking water for every member of your family is critical in any disaster or survival situation. While stocking up on bottled water beforehand is the best assurance that you will have what you need, you must also be prepared to find other sources and have the equipment and know-how to purify questionable water before using it. Your stored supply may be insufficient for the duration of the event, or you may be cut off from home or forced to bug out or evacuate on short notice with no means to carry enough to sustain you. Your knowledge of purifying water should include both primitive methods with no special equipment and the use of filters and other modern aids. Finding surface water will be easy enough in most places, but if your home is in an arid region, learning where to look for water in desert conditions is a must as well. See page 61 for more on water purification methods.

2. LEARN TO BUILD A TEMPORARY SHELTER

If you are caught out in the open away from your home or other permanent shelter, or have to move quickly with no tent, tarp or other portable shelter, it is essential that you know how to utilize available materials around you to make a temporary shelter. Those materials may be anything from manmade debris, such as scraps of building material, plastic or cardboard, to natural materials found in the wild, such as grasses, tree branches, bark or leaves. Studying the primitive shelters used by indigenous people around the world is a good place to start when it comes to using natural materials in a given region. Primitive living and survival courses can provide hands-on instruction in this kind of shelter making.

3. LEARN TO BUILD A FIRE IN ADVERSE CONDITIONS

The ability to quickly build a fire could be the difference between life or death in many situations, especially in cold, windy and wet conditions that make doing so more difficult. It is essential that you practice your fire-building skills beforehand and that you know from experience how and where to find dry wood in the rain, how to prepare your materials and keep the fire fueled, and how to start it with matches and alternative methods. In addition to warmth, fire offers light, a way to purify water and a way to cook foods that would otherwise be inedible. You can teach yourself and practice on weekend camping trips or learn from experts in survival courses. The ultimate fire-building skill is to learn to use the bow drill or other primitive methods to make fire without matches.

4. LEARN TO NAVIGATE ON LAND AND WATER

The ability to find your way is critical in an emergency, when conventional, marked routes such as streets and highways may be unusable or unsafe for travel. You must be able to navigate cross-country if necessary, and if rivers, lakes or seashores are part of your geographic region and you may need to travel on them, you should know how to navigate by water as well. Orienteering, cross-country hiking and small boat paddling or sailing are good ways to get experience with using a compass, as well as natural landmarks, the sun and the stars to find your way.

5. LEARN FIRST AID AND NATURAL REMEDIES

The ability to quickly and correctly administer first aid to injured companions, family members or even yourself can be the difference between life and death. Minor and serious injuries are common in disaster scenarios, and treating wounds effectively without outside help requires knowledge that will take time and study to acquire. The time to begin learning is now. A good place to start is a basic first aid certification course. Advanced course such as the Wilderness Advanced First Aid training offered by NOLS (National Outdoor Leadership Schools, www.nols.edu) would be even better.

6. LEARN UNARMED AND ARMED CLOSE-QUARTERS FIGHTING SKILLS

While firearms are certainly the preferred choice in dangerous confrontation, the fact remains that no matter how skilled you are in their use and how diligent you are in keeping a gun on hand and at the ready, there is no way you can be certain of always having one available. Self-defense training both with and without weapons can give you a decided advantage in a confrontation. Acquiring these skills will require dedicated practice with a partner or multiple partners, and the guidance of a good instructor. In most areas you can find classes in a variety of disciplines, from traditional martial arts to boxing, mixed martial arts or modern military combat methods such as Krav Maga.

7. LEARN TO USE FIREARMS FOR PERSONAL AND HOME DEFENSE, AS WELL AS HUNTING

The ability to use firearms of all types should be high on your list of skills to acquire if you are not already proficient with them. Begin with firearms safety courses and progress to more advanced courses in marksmanship and defensive and combat shooting. In addition to competent instruction, there is no substitute for range time to improve your shooting abilities. Hunting with firearms also requires excellent marksmanship, and sport hunting can provide valuable experience in the field that can prepare you for times when you really need firearms skills to survive.

8. LEARN TO IDENTIFY, GATHER AND PREPARE WILD PLANT FOODS

If you know what to look for, wild plant foods are generally easier to find and more abundant than animal foods and do not require special equipment to gather them. No matter which region of the country you live in, there are almost always some wild plant foods available, even in winter. While they may not be present in large enough quantities to sustain you long term, wild edibles can certainly be a supplement to your stored foods and to animal foods you can collect by hunting, fishing or trapping.

9. LEARN TO HUNT, TRAP, FISH AND COLLECT OTHER ANIMAL FOODS

If you did not grow up in an area where hunting and fishing was a major extracurricular activity or pastime, you will have a big learning curve ahead of you to gain the skills needed to successfully harvest game and fish in the wild. The best way to learn is to go with others who are more experienced. But while hunting typical game animals and fishing for species like bass or trout may be difficult at first, you should also consider the other, less-desirable small birds, reptiles, amphibians, aquatic creatures and insects found in your region, as these can often be easier to catch while still providing valuable protein.

10. LEARN TO MAINTAIN AND REPAIR ESSENTIAL GEAR AND EQUIPMENT

This may be one of the most overlooked skill sets of all, but it is an important part of self-reliance, both in normal times and in times of disaster and survival. Gear and equipment requiring maintenance and repair includes things like camp stoves, generators, chainsaws, firearms and all sorts of vehicles from cars and trucks to motorcycles, ATVs, bicycles and watercraft. In addition to these items requiring mechanical and/or electrical tools and skills, maintenance and repair also includes leatherwork, sewing and other handcrafts needed to maintain boots, backpacks, clothing, etc. Rebuilding, fixing and making as much of your own gear as possible while assembling your preps is a great way to learn these skills, and doing so will give you a great sense of self-sufficiency in the face of a possible long-term disruption of normal life.

Section 2
SPECIFIC-THREAT PREPPING

Chapter 5:
TORNADOES AND SEVERE STORMS

Tornadoes are certainly among the most frightening of natural disasters, not only because of their horrific intensity, but because they can develop, move fast and strike almost from out of nowhere with little or no warning, making them hard to avoid or prepare for. Hidden in the driving rain of a thunderstorm, you may not even be able to see an approaching tornado, especially if it occurs at night. Because of the short warning time, if you have any warning at all, there is little you can do to protect your home or property from destruction if a direct hit from a strong twister is imminent. In this circumstance, you and your family may be lucky to escape with your lives.

Tornadoes have been observed on every continent except for Antarctica, but are far more common in North America, especially the regions in the eastern half of the continent (see the map opposite). Within this larger region are many areas that suffer a higher frequency of tornadoes and severe storms. The first line of defense against these killer storms is to study historical weather data to determine if the area in which you live is particularly prone to tornado activity, then understand how tornadoes form and what kind of weather conditions, such as frontal systems and strong thunderstorm cells, can spawn them.

Tornado and severe thunderstorm forecasting has gotten more accurate in recent years with the widespread use of accurate weather radar systems. While a tornado can spawn quickly, the radar can show areas of intense activity where conditions are favorable for tornado development. If you have access to a television or the Internet via a computer or a smartphone,

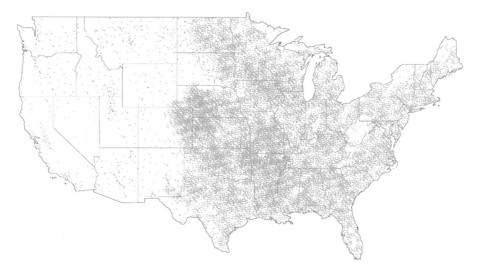

Reported Tornado Events Through U.S. History. While no state in the continental United States is free of tornado danger, the vast majority of deadly and severe twisters touch down east of the Oklahoma Panhandle. *(Source: National Oceanic and Atmospheric Administration)*

you can view live radar imagery for your area and see if you are in a tornado watch area or if a tornado warning (meaning a twister has been spotted) has been issued and you are in its path.

In some cases, you may know many hours or even a day or two in advance if your area is likely to be hit with tornado activity associated with large-scale storm systems that typically move across North America from west to east. Depending on the surface and upper-level air temperatures both ahead of and behind such a system, forecasters can often predict whether or not tornadoes are likely to form as the storm moves across your region.

Keeping track of the weather and monitoring the broadcasts on TV or with a receiver that can pick up NOAA (National Oceanic and Atmospheric Administration) Weather Radio forecasts is your best defense against getting caught off guard by a fast-moving twister. Be aware too that even if a tornado does not form, many strong frontal systems can pack straight-line winds in excess of hurricane force, as well as damaging hail up to softball size and deadly lightning.

UNDERSTANDING HOW TORNADOES ARE GENERATED

Most tornadoes form from thunderstorms, and the reason the central and eastern parts of the U.S. are more favorable to their development is the convergence of warm, moist air from the Gulf of Mexico with cool, dry air from Canada, which creates atmospheric instability. Merging air temperatures at different levels creates updrafts and downdrafts that can lead to large, invisible rotations within a thunderstorm, which sometimes become the compact vortices that reach the ground and become tornadoes.

The most extreme tornadoes can have wind speeds of 300 miles per hour, can be as wide as two miles and can stay on the ground for several miles. However, winds around 110 miles per hour or less are more common, and most tornadoes dissipate quickly.

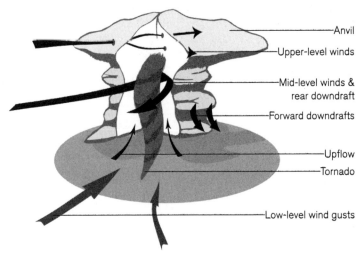

The anatomy of tornado formation in a supercell storm cloud.

ACTIVITY 5.1: **IS YOUR HOME IN THE PATH OF A TWISTER?**

Research the tornado history of your local area (as well as where you work, where your kids go to school, where your favorite vacation place is, etc.) online. There are numerous sites you can do this on, including Weather Underground Data History and Archive (www.wunderground .com/history); NOAA's National Weather Service National Climate (www.nws.noaa.gov /climate); The Old Farmer's Almanac Weather History (www.almanac.com/weather); National Climatic Data Center (www.ncdc.noaa.gov); Weather.org World Weather Forecast and Climate History (weather.org); Past Weather—NOAA (www.noaa.gov.pastweather.html).

It may have been decades since a twister touched down in your town or city, but the historical results are bound to shock you.

ACTIVITY 5.2: TEN SIMPLE STEPS TO INCREASING A HOME'S SURVIVAL IN A TORNADO

1. **Trim shrubs and trees around your house.** Make sure to remove dead or diseased branches or entire trees or bushes if they are suspect. Large branches and falling trees are often the cause of fatalities in strong storms and tornadoes.

2. **Secure outdoor furniture and other items for the duration of storm season.** Whether you're chaining you're your patio table or putting away gardening tools in the shed, this simple exercise can save a lot of damage from happening, especially if the items are near glass windows or patio doors. Almost any object, even things as large as vehicles, can become flying projectiles in the strongest tornadoes, but you can reduce risk of extra damage from flying objects in lesser events.

3. **Replace landscaping gravel and small rocks with shredded bark or other soft material.** Landscaping gravel may look nice, but in a storm with 200-mile-an-hour winds, that gravel will turn into thousands of dangerous tornado-blown bullets.

4. **Consider installing tornado roofing.** Roofing rated as Class 3 or 4 by UL 2218 or FM 4473 have been proven to better withstand hail damage, the other leading cause of damage from these storms, than standard-grade roofing.

5. **Secure top-heavy furniture such as bookcases to the walls.** A couple of easy-to-install brackets will reduce the chances of tall, unsteady furniture pieces from toppling over and injuring someone. (Just before a storm, if there is time, move furniture away from windows).

6. **Identify the safest existing area/room in your house or apartment.** This should be a small room without windows, such as a bathroom, closet, hall or stairwell in the middle of the structure and on the lowest floor level. The idea is to put as many walls as possible between you and the storm, and smaller rooms or spaces are also better able to withstand collapsing forces from above, such as a falling tree or roof structure.

7. **Build a reinforced safe room.** You can improve the protection offered by a small interior room by purposefully reinforcing it to create a safe room. To do this, reinforce the connections of the room's framing to the foundation or floor joists of the house, reinforce the connections of the adjoining wall framing and ceiling joists, and sheath the walls with structural lumber or plywood rather than the lightweight paneling or drywall typical of interior rooms. The door(s) to the safe room should also be extra heavy and hung with heavy-duty hinges and fitted with secure deadbolt locks.

8. **Install or build an underground tornado shelter.** Because the fury of the wind in a powerful tornado is so devastating, the best refuge is below ground. If you are lucky enough to have a basement, a reinforced safe room built inside it is a simple option. If

retreating below your house is not possible, you can build or buy a pre-made tornado shelter that can be situated below ground in the yard nearby. If you live in an area with a high likelihood of tornadoes, this is a worthwhile investment for peace of mind.

9. **Prepare to bug out.** Identify escape routes from all areas of your home and check to see if you need any special equipment such as a rope ladder.

10. **Prepare a 72-hour storm kit.** As in all disasters, having a minimum three-day supply of the essentials will enable you to meet the basic needs of you and your family members in the aftermath when help may not be able to reach you. (Complete the checklist in the following section to prepare your kit.)

ACTIVITY 5.3: BUILDING A TORNADO-SPECIFIC STORM SURVIVAL KIT

The contents of a tornado-specific storm survival kit will be similar to the 72-hour emergency kits in this book, except that because of the quick-forming and fast-moving nature of this particular disaster, you will not be evacuating in advance of the event, as you would in a hurricane, for instance. Instead, the focus when preparing this kit should be on including what you will need for you and your family in the hours immediately after the storm if your home is destroyed or badly damaged, utilities such as electricity, gas and phone communications are down, and roads are impassable because of fallen trees. In most cases, because tornado disasters are limited in geographical scope, outside help in the form of search-and-rescue teams will arrive well before 72 hours. Nevertheless, you should plan to be self-sufficient for at least 24 hours, and your kit should be built around providing temporary shelter, first aid, food, water and emergency communications. Injuries are a real possibility for all tornado survivors, and even if uninjured, it may be difficult to leave, even on foot, because of the amount of debris. Plan to have what you need to comfortably camp out in your damaged home or backyard if your home is destroyed. If you plan to retreat to a safe room or underground tornado shelter, you should have these survival essentials inside the shelter area with you, as collapsed framing and other debris may trap you and your family inside until help arrives to dig you out.

TIPS & TRICKS

TORNADOES CAN ACCOMPANY HURRICANES AND TROPICAL STORMS

Spin-off tornadoes are a real threat anytime a tropical storm or hurricane makes landfall. These tornadoes frequently occur in the outer bands of the cyclone and can cause damage and destruction far from the area of damaging winds surrounding the eye wall.

24-HOUR TORNADO SURVIVAL KIT

- ☐ Tent or tarp for temporary shelter (for use after the danger has passed)
- ☐ Sleeping bags, blankets for each family member
- ☐ Enough drinking water for each family member (at least 1 gallon per person)
- ☐ Food: 24-hour supply of ready-to-eat high-energy foods and snacks
- ☐ Dried fruit
- ☐ Nuts, seeds
- ☐ Granola, cereal
- ☐ Crackers
- ☐ Jerky, canned or packaged meats
- ☐ Comfort foods (candy, chocolate, cookies, etc.)

- ☐ Hand-operated can opener
- ☐ Swiss Army knife or multitool
- ☐ Flashlights and spare batteries
- ☐ Emergency candles
- ☐ Butane lighters and/or matches
- ☐ Rain jackets or ponchos
- ☐ Cell phone with extra battery or battery-powered charger
- ☐ Battery-powered hand-held CB, VHF or other emergency transmitter to aid searchers in finding shelters buried under debris
- ☐ Battery-powered weather radio receiver
- ☐ First aid supplies including wound dressings, antibiotic ointments, pain relievers and prescription medications

HAVE A PLAN FOR OUTSIDE THE HOME

Check the places you and your family routinely spend a lot of time and find out what the tornado plan and safe areas for those places are. These include schools, workplaces, sports facilities, churches, theaters, shopping centers and malls.

WHAT TO DO BEFORE AND DURING A TORNADO THREAT

Stay informed on your local weather conditions. TV and online weather sites will let know if you are in the path of a storm. As already mentioned, live radar images can be your best aid in determining if your home is in the path of a tornado. Radio is the next best option, and when the power fails and telephone and cell service is down, a battery-powered radio that can receive NOAA weather radio broadcasts is the most reliable means of staying informed.

Stay alert and observe changing weather conditions. Rapidly darkening or greenish skies and low-lying thunderstorm clouds are especially dangerous. Hail sometimes precedes tornadoes in a storm system, and you may hear the freight train–like roar of a tornado even if you can't see it because of the rain or darkness.

If your home is in the path of a tornado, get in your tornado shelter or safe room if you have one. If you don't have a tornado shelter or safe room, go into the basement or smallest space in the interior of the house, away from exterior walls (closet, under stairs, bathroom, hall, etc.). Do not open windows.

If you are in a trailer or mobile home, get out and try to make your way to a substantial building or to a ditch or other depression in the landscape. Mobile homes offer no protection from a tornado.

ODDS OF SURVIVAL IN AN F5 TORNADO

Fortunately, the strongest tornadoes are also quite rare. F3 and stronger tornadoes account for only about 6 percent of all tornadoes, but 75 percent of tornado deaths. F5 tornadoes are extremely rare, as are survivors who suffer a direct hit from them. The odds of living through such an experience are extremely low unless one is underground in a strong and properly built tornado shelter. In tornadoes of this category, a basement or open underground shelter is not enough.

SURVIVAL IN THE AFTERMATH OF A TORNADO

- If possible, continue to monitor your battery-powered radio for updates and emergency information.

- If a tornado has damaged your home, be wary of broken gas lines in the aftermath. Do not light candles inside if there may be ruptured gas lines. If you smell gas, turn off the gas lines and leave the house immediately.

- If your power service line is down or you see exposed, broken wiring in the house, or see sparks or smell burning, shut off your main circuit breakers if you have not already done so.

- Wear sturdy shoes or boots if you must move around in the debris. Broken glass, protruding nails, splintered wood and other hazards will be everywhere.

- Do not use generators, portable camp stoves, propane grills, heaters or other carbon-monoxide-producing devices inside your home, not even by an open door, window or in the garage.

WATERSPOUTS ARE TORNADOES OVER WATER

Although many waterspouts are small and short-lived, they are not to be taken lightly, especially if you are caught out in the path of one in a boat. Wind speeds of up to 190 miles per hour have been recorded in large waterspouts. Waterspouts are so common in the waters around the Florida Keys that estimates put their occurrence there at around 400 to 500 per year. Some researchers suspect a number of Bermuda Triangle boat-disappearances can be attributed to waterspouts. These tornadoes forming over water can also move ashore and can occur off the Atlantic and Pacific coasts, as well as the Gulf of Mexico and Great Lakes.

TORNADO SURVIVAL OUTSIDE OF THE HOME

- If you are caught outside when a tornado is approaching, get into your car if possible and drive to the nearest substantial building. If you are in an urban area or any area with lots of congestion, do not attempt to escape the tornado in your car. Get out of the car and into a building.

- If you are caught in your car out on the open road and no safe building is nearby, don't attempt to directly outrun the tornado. If possible, drive away from its path at a perpendicular angle to get out of the line of danger.

- If you are unable to drive out of the path in time and your vehicle is being hit with flying debris, pull over and park, and get down to the floorboards of the car, pulling a blanket, coat or cushions over you if possible.

- If there is a nearby ditch or other depression lower than the roadway and you are not in immediate danger of being hit by debris, leave the vehicle and get as low as possible, lying flat and covering your head with your hands if nothing else if available. This is also best strategy if you are out in the open on foot with no vehicle. Try to find the lowest spot in the vicinity, away from trees and other objects that can fall on you, and stay down until the danger passes. Getting struck by flying or falling debris causes most fatalities in tornadoes.

TORNADOES CAN OCCUR AT ANY TIME

Most tornadoes occur between 3 and 9 p.m., but can occur at any time of day or night. In the southern states, peak activity is from March through May, while farther north, late June through August is the highest-risk part of the year.

ACTIVITY 5.4: TORNADO DRILL PRACTICE MAKES PERFECT

Now that you've fully prepared for a tornado event, it's important to practice your emergency protocol with the whole family. In tornado-prone areas, tornado drills are sometimes conducted in schools or the workplace. You can conduct similar drills at home so you can be sure that everyone in the family knows exactly what to do when seconds count. After making sure everyone knows where to go and what to do and what not to do, you can proceed with the drill by announcing a tornado warning as if you just received one on the radio or TV weather report, or heard your community's tornado warning siren.

- The drill coordinator should announce the tornado warning by going from room to room, making sure everyone in your house is alerted.

- Everyone in the family should make their way to the predetermined safest area of the house, or the safe room or tornado shelter if there is one.

- The tornado survival supplies you have prepared in the checklist given in this chapter should be already in place or brought to the safe area or shelter at this time and inspected to be sure all necessities are included.

- During a real tornado, everyone in the room should crouch down as low to the floor as possible, facing down and covering their heads with their hands. You can practice this now.

- After everyone is in position, the drill coordinator can announce the threat has passed and then everyone should participate in discussing problems or concerns revealed by the drill and ways to improve readiness in a real tornado.

TIPS & TRICKS

INVOLVE YOUR NEIGHBORS

Talk to your neighbors about their tornado plan and discuss potential problems or dangers such as large trees near property lines and residents with special needs who might need help getting to shelter. If possible, organize neighborhood preparedness meetings to discuss emergency plans.

Chapter 6:
TROPICAL STORMS AND HURRICANES

Unlike tornadoes and severe thunderstorms, unless you live on an island with no connection to the outside world, you should have plenty of warning that a tropical cyclone or hurricane is threatening. In North America, the National Hurricane Center closely monitors all weather activity in the tropics during hurricane season, zeroing in on areas where conditions are right to spawn tropical depressions, tropical storms and, ultimately, hurricanes.

Once a storm is named, its path will be tracked and continuously monitored, with regular updates increasing in frequency if it becomes a full hurricane and especially if it threatens land. Hurricane tracking and prediction has certainly improved, but many factors can contribute to a storm altering course or increasing in intensity, sometimes just before it makes landfall.

The safest plan for hurricane avoidance is to leave the coastal area entirely, but in lower-intensity storms, especially if the path is not likely to make a direct hit or pass your location in a way that puts you on the intense side of the storm, it may be better to stay put rather than join the many less prepared people who will gridlock the roads in their panic. If you do leave, it should be early—well before all those last-minute evacuees hit the roads. Living in a coastal hurricane zone requires constant vigilance and a well-thought-out plan, along with the supplies you need to execute it.

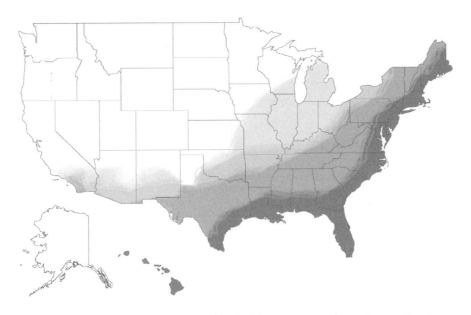

The United States effected by hurricanes through history. The NOAA has tracked hurricanes for more than 150 years. During that time, only a small handful of states have escaped the path, and thus the effects, of a major tropical storm. So, no matter where you live, it's better safe than sorry. *(Source: National Oceanic and Atmospheric Administration)*

HURRICANE SURVIVAL ESSENTIALS FOR THOSE IN POTENTIAL HURRICANE ZONES

1. Stay on top of the tropical weather forecast during hurricane season.

2. Have an evacuation plan and keep your vehicle in good repair and full of fuel.

3. Have a 72-hour kit (see checklist on page 122) ready to go at all times.

4. Don't attempt to ride out a direct hit from a major (Category 3 or higher) hurricane or lose time leaving trying to save possessions.

5. If you do stay at home for a lesser hurricane threat, be prepared to be completely self-sufficient in the aftermath, with everything you need for many days or even weeks.

6. If you are caught outside in the storm, take shelter indoors or in a ditch away from flying debris that can be deadly when driven by high winds.

7. If you are in already in a house or building, stay away from windows and retreat to the smallest spaces, such as halls or bathrooms.

8. Don't be fooled by the calm in the eye of the storm. When it passes over you can expect winds of the same intensity as before, but from the opposite direction.

9. Don't get trapped inside a building by the storm surge; get outside and make your way to the roof. If you are swept away, try to use any floating debris for buoyancy.

10. Proceed with caution in the aftermath; be aware of downed power lines, gas leaks, sharp objects and displaced dangerous animals like snakes and alligators.

TIPS & TRICKS

FALLING TREES ARE A MAJOR CAUSE OF FATALITIES

Major hurricanes cause death and destruction far inland, well beyond the reach of the storm surge, and falling trees are often the cause. It may not be practical or desirable to remove all the trees on your property that are close enough to fall on your house, but if you have such trees, consider sheltering elsewhere. Deaths from falling trees sometimes occur hundreds of miles from the coastline in the path of a strong hurricane.

ACTIVITY 5.1: **CHECKLIST FOR BUILDING A HURRICANE-SPECIFIC SURVIVAL KIT**

This 72-hour emergency kit differs from the bug-out bag discussed elsewhere in this book. This is a three-day kit to enable you to comfortably wait out a storm or other disaster, whether at home or while evacuating to a shelter or home of a relative or friend outside of the effected area. Unlike in a bug-out situation, you won't likely be retreating to an uninhabited area or attempting to forage from the land with the 72-hour kit. Its purpose is to make you self-sufficient until the power is restored, help arrives or you can relocate to a safer area. It can be assembled in a backpack just or be part of your regular bug-out bag, or you can keep the contents in a box or other container in your home, the trunk or your car or wherever you are sure that they will be available to you when needed.

TIPS & TRICKS

DON'T GET TRAPPED BY THE SURGE

If you are caught in a house or other building in a rising storm surge, don't get trapped on an upper floor or attic with no way out. Get outside before the water rises too high and make your way to the roof. Many people drowned inside rooms and attics in the storm surge of Hurricane Katrina.

HURRICANE SURVIVAL CHECKLIST

Water

(3 gallons per person—this minimum amount allows 1 gallon per person per day for all drinking and cooking needs)

- [ ] Base water supply
- [ ] Water filter or purification tablets to treat additional water as needed

Food

(Three-day supply of items that can be eaten without cooking)

- [ ] Dried fruit (raisins, banana chips, apples, mango, etc.)
- [ ] Nuts, seeds (almonds, cashews, sunflower seeds, pumpkin seeds, etc.)
- [ ] Granola
- [ ] Crackers
- [ ] Jerky
- [ ] Canned or packaged meats (tuna, sardines, chicken, etc.)
- [ ] Vegetables and fruits (like carrots, apples, oranges, bananas)
- [ ] Comfort foods (hard candy, chocolate bars or M&Ms, cookies, etc.)

Supplies

- [ ] Basic utensils
- [ ] Manual can opener
- [ ] Set of fork, knife, spoon for each person
- [ ] Cup, bowl and/or plate for each person
- [ ] Swiss Army knife or multitool
- [ ] Flashlight and spare batteries
- [ ] Emergency candles
- [ ] Fire starters (butane lighters, waterproof matches, and alternative method such as FireSteel)
- [ ] Shelter: 8x10-foot tarp as a minimum shelter, or a tent if more protection from weather or insects is needed
- [ ] Sleeping bag or fleece blanket depending on conditions/climate
- [ ] Clothing
- [ ] Outer rain/wind protection
- [ ] Extra under layers
- [ ] Socks, etc., as needed for conditions/climate

TIPS & TRICKS

STORM SURGE CAN REACH UNPRECEDENTED LEVELS

Never underestimate the danger potential of rising storm surge waters in a large hurricane. Many of the victims of Hurricane Katrina on the Mississippi coast died because they thought the 27-foot storm surge of Hurricane Camille in 1969 was the worst that could ever occur. In Bay St. Louis and Waveland, Mississippi, Katrina's surge reached an incredible 35 feet above normal sea level. Storm surge is greatest when hurricanes move ashore in areas where shallow water extends for miles beyond the coastline.

HURRICANE SURVIVAL CHECKLIST

Protection

(A handgun or other firearm may be part of your 72-hour kit, but keep in mind that if you are evacuating to a shelter you won't be allowed to keep it.)

- ☐ Firearms
- ☐ Pepper spray

Communications

- ☐ Cell phone
- ☐ Extra battery or battery-powered charger
- ☐ Battery- or crank-powered weather band radio receiver

Hygiene

- ☐ Toothbrush (for each person)
- ☐ Toothpaste
- ☐ Toilet paper
- ☐ Hand sanitizer
- ☐ Soap
- ☐ Feminine hygiene needs

First Aid

- ☐ Pain relievers
- ☐ Antidiarrheal tablets
- ☐ Antibiotic ointment
- ☐ Allergy creams
- ☐ Personal prescriptions
- ☐ Bandages
- ☐ Tape

Miscellaneous

- ☐ Emergency contact list
- ☐ Emergency cash in small denominations
- ☐ Duct tape
- ☐ Sunglasses
- ☐ Books or e-book reader
- ☐ Deck of cards or other entertainment such as portable MP3 player

ACTIVITY 5.2: TEN SIMPLE HOME PROJECTS TO PREPARE YOUR HOME FOR HURRICANE SEASON

1. **Get ready to batton the hatches.** Taping glass does not prevent it from breaking. Instead, take the time now to install hurricane shutters or, if you're looking to save money, cut and fit plywood covers to each window. This activity can be done in a weekend with a tape measure and a trip to Home Depot. Don't forget to label each plywood piece with markings like "Master Bedroom Window—Left"; that way they're ready to install quickly and securely when the time comes. Don't forget to do the same for large glass panes in doors and especially vulnerable sliding glass patio doors.

2. **Lock the doors.** On Saturday morning, make a full inspection of each exterior door on your home. Make sure each door has at least three hinges strongly fastened to the

framing and that there is at least one deadbolt lock on each door with a bolt measuring no shorter than 1 inch in length.

3. **Check the roofing.** A quick climb onto the roof will give you a chance to check for any missing or damaged shingles that could turn into a leak, or worse, a full-on hole during a major storm. Replace any damaged shingles or coverings well before storm season begins. If installing a new roof, be sure that you or your roofing company removes all old coverings down to the wood sheathing and replaces any damaged or weakened areas of sheathing.

4. **Fasten the roof to the house.** If you have an attic in your house or exposed roof rafters, make sure each rafter is secured to the frame of the house using hurricane clips or similar durable bracing ties. If you think this is overkill, just remember back to all the roofless houses in the aftermath of Hurricane Andrew. Even if your roof isn't going to blow off, the ties will help reduce basic damage to the roof during a storm.

5. **Fortify your garage.** Reinforce your garage doors by installing extra sliding bolts or other latch systems to make sure they stay down. Install wood or metal stiffeners on large garage doors, which are particularly vulnerable. Wind entering a garage can build up tremendous pressure.

TIPS & TRICKS

THE POWER OF A CATEGORY 5 HURRICANE

Sustained wind speeds of 157 miles per hour or greater cause total destruction or irreparable damage to most homes and buildings other than the most heavily reinforced or best engineered structures. Nearly all trees, power-line poles and signs will be blown down or broken. Power outages and water shortages will render effected areas uninhabitable for weeks or months.

- **Prepare a safe harbor from the outdoors.** Figure out a place inside where you will be able to quickly secure all outdoor furniture, garbage cans, decorations or anything else that is not tied down and could become a projectile in high winds. This may mean making a little extra room in the garage.

- **Cut the foliage.** Trim trees and shrubs around your home, making sure to remove dead or weakened branches. Diseased or other suspect trees near the house should be removed before a storm strikes. Other than drowning in the storm surge zone, falling trees and large branches are the most likely cause of fatalities in hurricanes.

- **Gut your gutters.** Repair loose gutters and downspouts and clear them of leaves and debris. The amount of rainfall generated in just a few hours by a hurricane may exceed you're your area would typically experience in an entire season or even year. Backed-up gutters and downspouts can cause roof damage and leaking, as well as foundation damage.

- **Let there be light (and fans and AC).** Take some time to shop for and consider installing a fixed generator if you anticipate needing more power than a portable can provide. Plan your fuel needs and safe fuel storage location. Living without fans or air conditioning in Florida or many other hurricane-prone areas of the South can be brutal during the times of the year most storms occur.

- **Plan for your vehicles.** During Superstorm Sandy, numerous residents of both New Jersey and New York risked their lives in order to move their cars as the flood waters came in. Don't leave your vehicles' fate (and possibly your own) for the last minute. Determine the safest place to park your vehicles, RVs, trailerable boats, etc., on high ground and away from overhanging trees, and move them to another storage location if necessary. Use the space below to draw or paste in a map of the ideal location and how to get there from your house.

HURRICANES CAN PRODUCE MASSIVE INLAND FLOODING

Aside from the coastal flooding caused by the rapid rise of sea water in the storm surge, the heavy rains that accompany hurricanes often create flash floods and other rising waters far inland. Big, slow-moving hurricanes are the worst for this, sometimes dumping rain at the rate of 6 inches per hour. In the mountainous Caribbean islands and coastlines of Central America, flash floods and mudslides account for a large percentage of hurricane fatalities.

ACTIVITY 5.3: CHECKLIST FOR SECURING YOUR VALUABLES AND HOME BEFORE EVACUATION

If you end up having to evacuate, it is unlikely you will be able to carry all your valuables with you when you leave. You will have to prioritize and decide which things are most important. The items in your 72-hour kit are a given. This checklist is for additional, non-survival items such as valuables and sentimental items that you may have room for in your vehicle along with all your family members and needed gear and supplies.

Many people living in hurricane-prone areas keep open or enclosed utility trailers for this purpose, or if you have a boat on at trailer the boat can also be filled with additional items if you are taking it with you anyway. Things that will be left behind should be secured and protected as well as possible. All of this is much easier if you plan ahead by filling out the following checklist so that in the stress of getting ready to evacuate, you will not have the burden of decisions getting in the way.

Go through your home room by room and identify such items and how they might fit in your available cargo space.

(If you have large items that can't be moved out of the hurricane zone in time, such as a boat that stays in a marina or an RV in a storage yard, you should also formulate a separate plan to deal with securing these items well in advance of leaving your home.)

DON'T BE FOOLED BY THE EYE OF A HURRICANE

If the wind suddenly stops, you may be in the temporary calm of the eye of the storm. This can last for up to several minutes depending on the hurricane's size and forward speed. When the eye passes over, you can expect winds of the same intensity as before, but from the opposite direction.

VALUABLE ITEMS TO EVACUATE CHECKLIST

- ☐ Personal computers/irreplaceable electronics
- ☐ Photo albums
- ☐ Important documents (birth certificates, passports, etc.)
- ☐ Cash/bonds/financial information
- ☐ Precious metals
- ☐ Jewelry
- ☐ Small family heirlooms
- ☐ Photography equipment
- ☐ Musical instruments
- ☐ Firearms

☐ _____
☐ _____
☐ _____
☐ _____
☐ _____
☐ _____
☐ _____
☐ _____
☐ _____
☐ _____
☐ _____

TIPS & TRICKS

DON'T RISK YOUR LIFE TO SAVE A BOAT

Large boats kept in the water are difficult to protect in hurricanes. Try to move the boat to a safe "hurricane hole" or haul it out before the storm. Many commercial fishermen died trying to save their boats (which were their livelihoods) in Hurricane Katrina, and recreational boat and yacht owners often take this risk as well. Remember that boats can be replaced.

HOMEOWNER'S INSURANCE: UNDERSTANDING WHAT IS AND IS NOT COVERED IN HURRICANE DISASTERS

Despite all your preparations to protect your home, severe damage or total loss is often the result if it is in the path of a hurricane. Insurance may be your only hope of financial recovery, but it is important that you understand what your policy does and does not cover. Many homeowners have been disappointed in the wake of major hurricanes upon learning that their standard policy does not cover the damage caused by water, which is often more destructive than the wind associated with these storms.

When storm surge levels are unprecedented, such as they were during Hurricane Katrina in 2005, homes far from the water or normal flood zones can be destroyed or severely damaged by rising water. A flood insurance policy added to your standard homeowner's policy is essential in such circumstances. After Katrina, there was much discussion as to whether homes were damaged by wind or water, whether the wind came before the water or vice versa, but the only safe bet is to have policies that cover damage from both forces.

For an explanation of what is and is not covered by flood insurance policies, see the section at the end of Chapter 7. In general, this type of insurance only covers water coming from outside your home (rising waters of a storm surge, for instance, and not broken water pipes).

For an explanation of what is and is not covered by flood insurance policies, see the section at the end of Chapter 7.

TIPS & TRICKS

MEASURING HURRICANE INTENSITY

The intensity of a hurricane is measured on the Saffir-Simpson Scale, which ranks hurricanes based on sustained wind speeds. When tropical storm winds reach 74 miles per hour, it is officially classed as a Category 1 hurricane. Category 2 begins at 96 miles per hour, Category 3 at 111 miles per hour, Category 4 at 130 and Category 5 at 157. The Saffir-Simpson Scale no longer includes central pressure or storm surge estimates, and also does not take the physical size and moving speed of the cyclone into effect. It is designed instead to indicate expected windspeeds and the resulting damage the wind will cause.

Chapter 7:
FLOODS, TSUNAMIS AND STORM SURGES

THE DANGERS OF RISING WATER

Since water covers over 70 percent of the earth's surface, chances are, regardless of where you live, you will, at some point, be directly or indirectly effected by a flood. Flooding is the most commonly occurring natural disaster in the world. When there is an overflow of an expanse of water (creek, pond, river, etc.) flooding occurs in all surrounding lower-lying areas. Floods can occur slowly over the course of several days or quickly with little or no warning, producing a flash flood. In fact, flooding is the most common weather-related hazard in the world, with flash flooding being the number-one weather-related killer. The danger is largely due to the fact that many people live in a flood plain, even if they do not realize it, and chances are you do too. It is just a matter of whether you live: in a low, moderate or high-risk area.

Annually, over three-quarters of declared federal disasters are the result of flooding, which means that flooding should be a part of your disaster preparation. The map on page 130 illustrates how prevalent flooding is in the United States. Your risk from a flood disaster at home is dependent on where you live in relation to nearby waters that could possibly reach your doorstep. The best course of action, if you do, would simply be to move somewhere else, if at all possible. If you choose not to, you must identify your risk and prepare.

Despite the risks, many homes are located in flood plains and remain safe from all but the most extreme events. If you do live in such a location, you must pay attention to flood watches and warnings and be prepared to evacuate. Even though the waters may not have reached your home, roads leading out of the area may become flooded first, cutting off your escape route. Driving through water covering a road is a dangerous proposition, as you may not be able to judge the depth of the water and the strength of the current. Your vehicle could easily be swept off the roadway by a modest amount of moving water.

TIPS & TRICKS

WADING ACROSS MOVING WATER

Use extreme caution when wading across moving water. Your feet can be swept out from underneath you in as little as six inches of fast moving water. Floodwaters will be murky and brown, and full of sediment and debris, making it impossible to judge depth, and hiding holes, drop-offs and underwater objects that can cause you to trip and fall.

HOW TO STAY SAFE DURING A FLOOD

The general rule for the possibility of flooding is that, at any given location, if it rains there, it can flood there, although there are locations that are far more likely to flood than others. Since flooding typically happens quickly and with little warning, your best odds to stay safe during a flood lie in preparation.

1. Inquire as to whether your home, job, school, and other important locations lie in a flood plain. By determining where they are in relation to flood plains, you can evaluate your risk and prepare accordingly.

2. Identify evacuation centers in your area and, in advance, map out multiple evacuation routes. Parts of your evacuation route may also be in a flood plain, so you will want to have options. In Activity 7.1 you will map out the best evacuation routes from your home, work, schools, etc. Drive the routes before the event happens, observe the terrain and consider possible obstructions and hindrances.

3. Check with your insurance agent to see if your home owner's policy covers flood damage. For more on flood insurance, see Understanding Flood Insurance (page 137).

4. Do what you can to flood-proof your home. Activity 7.2 guides you through some simple home projects that can help keep the water out.

5. Stay informed. Even though it may not be raining outside your window, at any given moment it could be raining upstream, causing your waterways to swell. Flood watches and warnings will be broadcast by local television and radio stations. When they are issued, evaluate your risk and, if necessary, take measures to ensure the safety of your family.

DEVASTATION OF THE HEARTLAND IN 1993: The Great Flood of 1993 was one of the most devastating floods in U.S. history. Flooding occurred in America's heartland from April until October. The Mississippi, Missouri, and Kansas rivers began spilling water over their banks in the spring and by the time the waters receded, the flooding had covered an area approximately 500 miles long and 200 miles wide and left over $15 billion in damages.

HOW TO SURVIVE A FLASH FLOOD

A flash flood is the rapid flooding of low-lying areas. Usually the flooding is of great volume but, fortunately, for a short duration, and is caused by heavy rainfall, sometimes hundreds of miles away. Flash flooding can occur on any body of water, but is most common along streams and creeks. Because many residential areas divert their water runoff by way of streams and creeks, highly populated areas are at risk of flash flooding. The speed and power of a flash flood can lead to devastating results. They are known to collapse buildings and bridges, sweep away trees and power poles, and erase roads from the map.

They best way to avoid a flash flood is to heed warnings. If a flash flood warning is issued or if you notice rapidly rising water, you should head for higher ground immediately. Drive, if possible, and be careful not to drive through standing or moving water. If your vehicle stalls due to floodwater, you should abandon it and evacuate quickly as long as you deem it safe to do so. The goal is to not get caught by the flash flood. Evacuate to higher ground as soon as possible.

If you are caught in the fast-moving water of a flash flood, the first rule—and the most difficult to follow—is don't panic. Remain calm in order to give yourself the best possible chances of escaping the current. Next, don't try to swim out of it. You will quickly become exhausted and be unable to rescue yourself. Float on the water on your back, with your head upstream and your feet in front of you. This will allow you to use your feet to deflect objects and lessen your chances of taking mouthfuls of water. Keep your head up to watch for objects, as well as slower-moving water near the shore. Look for eddies (circular-moving slow water on the downstream side of an object) that can give you enough protection to swim out of the current. Once you are in slower-moving water and close to a way out of the water, roll onto your stomach and swim upstream at a 45-degree angle toward your target. Turn and swim early because the current will continue to take you downstream as you get closer to your exit.

CHECK YOUR FOUNDATION GRADING

The dirt at your home's foundation should be a minimum of 6 inches higher than the dirt 6 feet away. You can make a simple gauge by cutting two lengths of wood: one 6 feet long and one 6 inches. Place the six food piece horizontally and nail the six inch piece to the end vertically (creating a sideways "L"). Place a level on the horizontal piece and you can determine if your lot is adequately graded away from your home.

ACTIVITY 7.1: MAPPING A FLOOD OR TSUNAMI ESCAPE ROUTE

Paste a topographical map of your area (including your home, offices, schools, etc.) and plan escape routes from each location to your designated "High Ground." An advanced evacuation plan inclusive of several options will offer you the best chance to quickly reach safety.

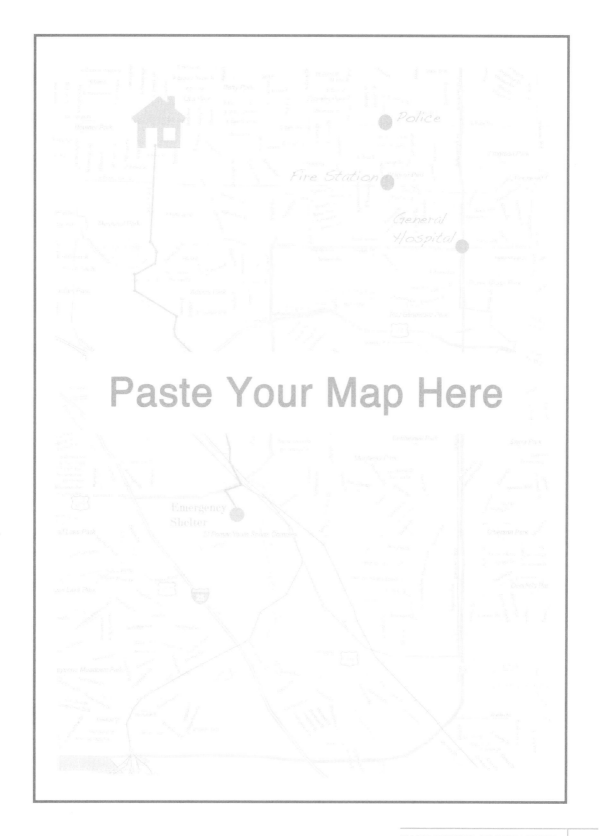

Paste Your Map Here

ALL FLOODWATERS ARE CONTAMINATED

Floodwaters carry a variety of bacteria and parasites. Ensure you are up to date on your immunizations and tetanus shots, and try to avoid contact with the water if you have any cuts or open sores in your skin. Chemicals and industrial pollutants will likely be present in floodwaters as well.

ACTIVITY 7.2: SIMPLE PROJECTS TO HELP YOUR HOME (AND POSSESSIONS) SURVIVE A FLOOD

1. Start with your gutters. Ensure that they are clean and free of debris. Install gutter guards to prevent accumulation of leaves, pine needles, sticks, etc. Gutters keep heavy rainfall from backing up and causing leaks in your roof or damaging your foundation around the perimeter of your house.

2. Install and maintain downspout extensions. Extend your downspouts at least six feet away from the home's foundation. If space doesn't allow for a downspout extension, install splash blocks to direct water away.

3. Seal the leaks. Holes and leaks should be sealed in your guttering, downspouts and downspout extensions. This can simply be done with a ladder and a tube of silicone. Also, a little more is involved, but cracks in the concrete (porch, sidewalks, driveway) around the home should be repaired or at the very least sealed.

4. One of the most important things you can do to keep unwanted water out of your home is to check the integrity of your foundation. If you notice cracks, consult a professional regarding repair.

5. If there has been erosion underneath your steps, patio or deck, grab a shovel and backfill it. Fill the empty space with dirt and grade it away from your foundation.

6. Install window wells where basement windows are at, near or below ground level. A window well is a U-shaped, ribbed, metal piece that allows space between ground level windows and the surrounding lot. They are available in various sizes, so measure your window to ensure you purchase the correct one. They are relatively easy to install. Consult a professional if you have any questions.

7. Check the grade of your lot. Your lot should be graded 4 to 6 inches down and away from your home and a minimum of 5 to 6 feet away. It is common for the ground around your foundation to erode, creating a depression. Add dirt to slope the ground away from your foundation. Be sure that you are not routing water away from your home and into your neighbor's house!

8. Install check valves in toilets, drains and other sewer connections to prevent flood-waters from backflowing into your home by way of water "exits." If you aren't a competent plumber, you should consult a professional.

TSUNAMIS AND STORM SURGES

Tsunamis are often referred to as "tidal waves," which is incorrect because they have nothing to do with the tides. The term "tsunami" conjures up images of towering waves reaching almost mythical proportions, but imagine a skyscraper-sized wave reaching up out of the sea and washing up several miles inland, causing monumental loss. While the threat of a tsunami is small compared to many other natural disasters, they are very real and can be astonishingly destructive. They frequently occur in the Pacific Ocean and are a result of an underwater disturbance such as an earthquake or volcanic eruption. A tsunami is not a single mammoth wave, but rather a series of large waves reaching as high as several stories. Even with current technology, it is nearly impossible to predict a tsunami, although once one is generated, forecasting the approximate time and location of impact is accurate.

Since the mid-1800s, tsunamis have been responsible for over 400,000 deaths. The 2004 tsunami that struck Indonesia and other nearby countries claimed over 200,000 of those lives. The threat of a tsunami is greatest if you live in specific geographical areas or near the coast, where the perilous waves can impact you. The states in the U.S. at the greatest risk for tsunamis are Hawaii, Alaska, Washington, Oregon, and California. Hawaii is under the greatest threat, typically receiving the brunt of one tsunami per year and a destructive tsunami about every seven years.

Keep in mind that just because you do not live on the Pacific Coast of the United States does not mean that you are free from tsunami threat. Some scientists have hypothesized that the next mega-tsunami may occur in the Canary Islands. The mega-tsunami (the term used to describe a tsunami caused by a landslide or impact event that creates larger than normal tsunami waves) could cross the Atlantic Ocean and devastate U.S. coastal cities like New York, Boston, and Miami. In addition, lakes around the world have experienced their own mini-mega-tsunamis caused by catastrophic landslides.

While some people compare the storm surges that accompany hurricanes to tsunamis, they are actually completely different in their formation, speed of movement and destructive force. A storm surge occurs when a tropical cyclone nears landfall, pushing large amounts of water ahead of it to create a gradual rise in sea level. If the surge coincides with areas of shallow water just off he coast and the normal high tide cycle, the resulting surge can be more than twenty feet above sea level. Unlike a tsunami, a storm surge does not come in as a single or series of fast-moving breaking waves. Nevertheless, the damage in the aftermath can appear similar because breaking, wind-driven waves on the surface of this higher level of water can reach structures normally far from the reach of waves. In Hurricane Katrina, the storm surge completely destroyed miles of four-lane highway bridges spanning St. Louis Bay and Back Bay of Biloxi.

ACTIVITY 7.3: **LEARN TO SURVIVE A TSUNAMI**

- Determine if there is a tsunami warning system in your area and if so what it includes.

- Pre-plan your escape route(s). (Activity 7.1)

- Know the telltale signs of a tsunami (especially for locations without adequate warning systems).

  Drawback. As a tsunami gathers water and strength it can "drawback" water from the coast, giving the appearance that the ocean is receding. Do not go down to the beach to admire the phenomenon. This is a warning and should alert you that evacuating is the best course of action.

  Animal flight. Hours before the Indian Ocean tsunami of 2004, large numbers of animals were seen heading for higher ground. Add this to your list of possible cues.

- Prepare an evacuation pack including essential survival and communication items that can be retrieved in a hurry for rapid escape.

- Be prepared to abandon your belongings. Property can be replaced, life cannot.

- Be prepared to bug out by foot. Reports have shown that people who attempt to evacuate in their cars are often caught in traffic jams or by other weather-related obstacles and are more likely to be caught by the waves. Evacuation on foot to higher ground may be the better, quicker and safer option.

- If you are caught in the water, do not try to swim out of it. Because of the enormous amount of dangerous debris in the water, you should try to get out of the water as quickly as possible. Grab a floating object that can keep you above water until you can self-rescue or help arrives.

- A tsunami can affect your ability to obtain food and taint and poison inland freshwater supplies. Take appropriate measures to ensure that you and your family have essential survival supplies until normal conditions return.

- Keep to high ground. Many tsunami-related casualties result from people going down to the coast after the first wave to offer assistance to those affected. Remember that a tsunami is a series of waves and that the next wave could be an hour away. Evacuate until authorities have given the OK to return.

UNDERSTANDING FLOOD INSURANCE

Understanding flood insurance first means to understand what a "flood" is as far insurance companies are concerned. There is a distinct difference between flood damage and water damage, and being able to discern between the two can carry significant financial implications. The distinction lies in the definition of a flood. According to the National Flood Insurance Program, a flood is "a general and temporary condition of partial or complete inundation of two or more acres of normally dry land area or of two or more properties (at least one of which is your property from: overflow of inland waters, unusual and rapid accumulation or runoff of surface waters from any source, and mudflows." This can be interpreted in a variety of ways, so it is important to get a clarification from your insurance company.

Some common examples of flooding are:
- Water from a nearby creek overflows its banks and washes into your home.

- Heavy rains saturate the ground, allowing water to seep into your basement.

- Flash flooding causes the ground from a nearby hill to give way, causing a mudslide that damages your home.

Some common examples of water damage are:

- A broken water pipe in your home.

- Heavy rains cause your roof to leak, allowing water inside and creating damage.

- A storm causes a tree branch to break a window, allowing rain inside your home.

Remember, homeowner's insurance and flood insurance are two separate things. Home-owner's insurance will typically cover water damage but not flood damage. Flood insurance will typically cover flood damage but not contents of the home. It is up to you to ask the right questions of your insurance agent to ensure that you are properly covered.

Some examples of questions you might ask are:

- What is the flood risk rating on my property?

- Is flood insurance required? Or recommended?

- Does my property qualify for a Preferred Risk Policy?

- What are the recommended coverage levels for the structure and contents?

- What premium discounts apply for this policy?

- What fees are applied to the annual flood insurance premium?

- How do Replacement Cost Value and Actual Cash Value affect the reimbursement amounts for my property?

- Who do I contact if a flood occurs?

A quick note about renter's insurance: Renter's insurance policies can be lengthy, confusing and somewhat vague, especially in the area of the flood coverage clause. One thing is certain: a standard renter's insurance policy will not cover flood damage. In this circumstance, the only way you will be actually protected from damage caused by a flood is if you take out a special policy that is only available through the National Flood Insurance Program (NFIP). There is no other way under a renter's insurance policy.

TIPS & TRICKS

FLASH FLOOD WATCH VS. FLASH FLOOD WARNING

A flash flood watch means that conditions are favorable for flash flooding. It is meant to raise aware-ness and allow you to begin preparing for the event. A flash flood warning occurs when a flood is occurring or imminent. Immediate action should be taken to protect lives and property.

Chapter 8:
EARTHQUAKES

The outermost layer of this great big planet of ours is made up of giant plates that move over, under and alongside each other. As those plates slip past one another along fractures, called fault lines, they release energy causing vibrations—an earthquake. Earthquakes are common and happen more often than most people realize; every day, to be exact. You can even check up-to-the minute earthquake occurrences at earthquake.usgs.gov/earthquakes. Most are not significant enough to be noticed, while others can be devastating. Often, after a large earthquake, several smaller ones, called aftershocks, can occur.

The West Coast of the United States is commonly thought of as being at the greatest risk for earthquakes. Despite the fact that California typically suffers the most earthquake damage, the state with the greatest number of earthquakes annually is actually Alaska, followed by California and then Hawaii. Earthquakes, though, are not exclusive to the western United States. They occur along fault lines throughout the country. For example, Missouri is that state with the sixteenth most earthquakes. The largest earthquakes felt in the United States were in Missouri along the New Madrid Fault in a series of quakes between 1811 and 1812. Several reached what would be over 8 on the Richter Scale (the logarithmic measurement of the amount of energy released by an earthquake, developed by Charles F. Richter in 1935). Those earthquakes were felt over the entire eastern United States.

You can determine your hazard risk by identifying your location on the map located in "Section 3: FEMA Earthquake Hazard Map" (www.fema.gov/earthquake/earthquake/hazard-maps). If you are in one of the identified areas that are at risk, you must be aware of the dangers that can occur when an earthquake hits and take the appropriate steps to ensure you are prepared.

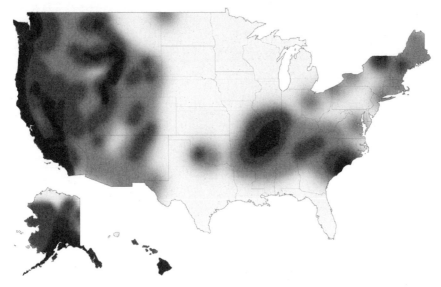

While most people think of the West Coast as "earthquake country," temblors can and have hit regions across the entire continent. *(Source: United States Geological Survey)*

With earthquakes come with a multitude of dangers, issues and secondary effects. Because there is no warning for an earthquake, escaping one is not an option. Preparation and reaction produce the best possible outcome. Before the earthquake happens, make sure you can locate and shut off water, electricity and gas to your home. The ability to shut off utilities gives you the ability to eliminate a variety of post event dangers.

TIPS & TRICKS

SLOWLY STOP AND PULL OVER

If you find yourself driving during an earthquake, you should pull safely off the road, stop the vehicle and set the parking brake. Try to avoid parking near bridges, overpasses, towers or even power lines, and stay in the vehicle. If a power line does fall on the vehicle, remain inside until it is removed by professionals.

IDENTIFYING AN EARTHQUAKE

What does an earthquake feel like anyway? An earthquake can be one of the most frightening events that you can experience. Your world shakes and you have no advance warning, no idea of how intense it will get, and no control of when it ends. The magnitude of earthquakes can vary greatly, ranging from a slight tremor to violent vibrations capable of crumbling buildings. The smaller earthquakes have been known to give the feeling of vertigo or a large vehicle passing by. The ground quivers and a slight rumble can often be heard. Larger quakes will cause you to sway, forcing you to grab on to an object to keep from falling over. The closer you are to the epicenter during an earthquake, the more violent and destructive it can be. Recognizing an earthquake isn't difficult. What you do before, during and after can make all the difference in the outcome.

CAN TOADS PREDICT EARTHQUAKES?

Some scientific evidence suggests that days before an earthquake, toads have the ability to sense seismic activity. In a study published by the *Journal of Zoology*, a pond in Italy was abandoned by 96 percent of the toads three days before an earthquake struck. Male toads, that typically remain at the breeding site until spawning is complete, did not return until ten days after the quake. The theory is debated equally on both sides, but in order to adequately study the possibility, ironically, the time and locations of earthquakes would have to be known in advance.

TIPS TO SURVIVING AN EARTHQUAKE

During the earthquake:

- Remain calm.

- If you are indoors, stay away from windows, mirrors, cabinets and shelves.

- Take cover under a sturdy table or desk while holding on to it.

- If there is nothing sturdy to protect you, stand against an interior wall. Avoid standing near exterior walls.

- Do not try to cover too much ground. Find a safe place very near where you are when the earthquake begins. Trying to walk or run to relocate could cause injury.

- If you are outside, avoid being near buildings, power lines, trees and anything else that could fall and cause injury.

- If you are driving, move the vehicle out of traffic and stop. Do not park it near bridges, overpasses, power lines or buildings.

After the earthquake:

- Be prepared for aftershocks to occur. During some events, the "aftershocks" can actually be more powerful than the initial earthquake itself.

- Identify if there are any injuries to you or your family.

- Locate hazards such as fire, electrical, water or natural gas. Shut off the sources if possible.

- Check for structural damage to your home.

- Be aware of broken glass and debris that could cause injury.

- Do not go near compromised trees, utility poles, chimneys or anything else that could fall on you.

- Stay out of damaged buildings.

- Keep the TV or radio (or crank radio) on for news reports. There may be important information on possible tsunamis (see Chapter 7) or fire outbreaks (see Chapter 10).

TIPS & TRICKS

EARTHQUAKES AND SPECIAL NEEDS

If someone in your home has special needs you may want to consider a close friend or relative to give a list of limitations, capabilities, and needs as well as a spare key.

ACTIVITY 8.1: ADD AN EARTHQUAKE PREPARATION KIT TO YOUR EXISTING SUPPLIES

Before the earthquake happens, make sure you can locate and shut off water, electricity and gas to your home. You can refer to the map you created in Chapter 1. As with all disasters, you may be forced to rely on whatever preparations you have made for survival or at least to sustain you until you can evacuate or help arrives. A well-stocked earthquake kit contains many of the same items that are contained in your other survival kits that you have built in this book. List the items below that you have in preparation for an earthquake. Remember that it is likely that emergency crews are inundated and will not be available, transportation may not be an option, and retrieving supplies from retail stores will not be possible. Some things to consider for your earthquake preparation kit are:

EARTHQUAKE SURVIVAL CHECKLIST

❏ Flashlights	❏ _____
❏ Batteries	❏ _____
❏ Radio	❏ _____
❏ Fire extinguisher	❏ _____
❏ First aid kit	❏ _____
❏ Food	❏ _____
❏ Water	❏ _____
❏ Manual can opener	❏ _____
❏ Appropriate weather protection	❏ _____

ACTIVITY 8.2: WEEKEND PROJECTS—SIMPLE PROJECTS TO HELP YOUR HOME SURVIVE A TREMOR

1. Secure Your Furniture

Walk through your home and identify furniture that might fall over during an earthquake. Smaller and lighter things such as floor lamps should not be of concern. Top-heavy furniture must be secured to a wall to prevent it from toppling over during an earthquake. Fasten an "L" bracket, corner bracket or another type of fastener to the wall at a stud. You can affix the furniture directly to the bracket or use something such as a nylon strap to attach the furniture to the bracket. There are also retail outlets that sell "earthquake straps" that claim to be able to hold objects such as furniture and televisions in place during a seismic event.

2. Keep Objects on Shelves in Place

A common trick in earthquake-prone areas is to string fishing line across the front of a shelf. The line is nearly invisible and it can prevent objects from sliding off and breaking or injuring someone. Move the heavier objects to lower shelves.

3. Install Fasteners on Cabinet Doors

Secure cabinet door latches are a great way to keep the objects located in the cabinets. This can be done on kitchen, bathroom, pantry, garage and all other household cabinets. A sliding bolt can be installed or, for a less obvious appearance, you can install childproof latches (that can serve a dual purpose if you have toddlers running around).

4. Securely Fasten Large Appliances

Large appliances can cause significant issues if they come loose from their affixed location. Water, electrical wires or natural gas dangers can become present and exposed when the appliances are damaged. Your water heater, furnace, washer, dryer, refrigerator and any other large appliances should be firmly affixed, using metal strapping, to a structural part of the house. Observe how your appliances are connected to water and gas. Consider using flexible water and gas attachments to your appliances to prevent a water or fire hazard.

5. Secure Small and Decorative Items

Some of the smaller items around your home can mean more to you than anything else. A family heirloom or a ceramic art project that your child made in kindergarten sometimes holds more value than your most expensive jewelry. One way to keep them in place and to protect them from minor to moderate earthquakes is to simply place small bits of wax or poster putty underneath them for traction.

6. Mind Your Hazardous Materials

Store flammable and caustic chemicals away from possible ignition sources or explosive appliances. The gas cans and pesticides in the garage are best kept in sealed containers on a low shelf in a lockable cabinet.

7. Keep Paths of Egress Clear

When an earthquake strikes, you need to ensure that you and your family can get away from danger as effortlessly as possible. One way to do this is to plan egress routes in your home and make sure there is nothing substantial that could hinder your evacuation. Walk the paths to your front and back doors, your stairs going up and down, and make sure you will be able to move about your home or get out as freely as you can.

TIPS & TRICKS

EARTHQUAKES IN THE U.S.

Earthquakes in the United States occur more frequently west of the Rocky Mountains but historically the most violent earthquakes happen in the central United States.

---

8. Plan Several Evacuation Routes

As with many of the other disasters mentioned in this book, you should have pre-planned evacuation routes. Remember that earthquakes alter the natural terrain. It is not uncommon to encounter structural collapse of homes and buildings, bridges, tunnels, railways, shipping ports and airports. Earthquakes are responsible for landslides, fires, flash flooding, tsunamis and sinkholes. Map out your evacuation routes and note the possible dangers that may hinder them.

9. Conduct Annual Earthquake Drills at Home and Work

If an earthquake were to occur, you should be prepared to protect yourself and your family. One of the most important ways to do this is to know what to do during an earthquake and to practice "duck, cover and hold" drills in your home, school or job. Practice and repetition of those drills will cause your reaction to an earthquake to be instinctively appropriate, rather than a panic-driven response. Discuss with your family the importance of recognizing that an earthquake is occurring. They should immediately drop to the floor, quickly crawl under a sturdy piece of furniture, then pull their knees into their chest and cover their head with their arms. If possible, they should put their back against an interior wall. Hold on to the furniture until the tremors stop. Conduct these drills often and discuss the structural and utility hazards that could be encountered after the earthquake.

TIPS & TRICKS

EARTHQUAKE INJURIES
Falling objects, broken glass and collapse are the cause of most earthquake-related injuries.

ACTIVITY 8.3: BIG PROJECTS TO CONSIDER

1. Bolt Your Home to the Foundation

Bolting your house to the foundation will help sturdy the structure in the event of an earthquake. This popular method is best left to licensed professionals and should typically not be considered a DIY-type of project. The sill plates (usually the lowest part of the wooden structure) are secured to the foundation with cast-in bolts. Once installed, the bolts can prevent your house from sliding off the foundation and, especially in earthquake- or hurricane-prone areas, can increase the value of your home.

2. Fortify a "Soft Story"

If your living quarters are built over an open first floor (like a garage or empty basement), your home is much more likely to collapse during a catastrophic earthquake. Soft stories are a hazard that present a significant risk to life safety and property damage during an earthquake. In order to fortify your home, there are kits that will strengthen the integrity of the first floor. Soft story seismic retrofitting adds structural components for buildings to remain standing during an earthquake. Many companies have the ability to fortify your soft story. Consult a professional.

3. Install Seismic Gas Shutoff Valves

During an earthquake, it is common for gas lines to rupture and for gas meters to be pulled away from houses, causing natural gas to leak and creating an explosive environment. Seismic gas shutoff valves are placed on the piping at your home's gas meter, and in the event that the meter pulls away from the house, the valve automatically shuts off the gas, eliminating the threat of a natural gas explosion. Use a licensed contractor to install seismic shutoff valves.

4. Consider Adding a Shear Wall to New Construction

If you live in an area with the potential for earthquakes, you may want to consider adding shear walls to the structure during construction. They are made of reinforced and heavily braced panels and are engineered to resist shear. "Shear" is the lateral force created by earthquakes that is responsible for the collapse of buildings, bridges, etc. Shear walls are not typically retrofit but are structural and included in the original construction. Architects in seismic areas should be familiar with shear walls and be able to assist you with design ideas that will offer structural stability while maintaining aesthetics.

TIPS & TRICKS

THE RING OF FIRE

The Ring of Fire is a horseshoe-shaped area in the Pacific Ocean that touches coastlines of North America, South America, China, Japan, and Russia. It is along this Ring of Fire that roughly 90 percent of the world's earthquakes occur.

Chapter 9:
WINTER STORMS

SURVIVING A WINTER WONDERLAND

Wintertime always brings its share of challenges. Along with the picturesque snow-blanketed landscapes comes treacherous terrain, cold-temperature-related medical issues and dangerous, icy conditions, to name a few. Extreme winter weather can affect the majority of the country and has the ability to make life difficult, even deadly, in the confines of your own home.

The potential danger of a winter storm varies greatly by region. Obviously the farther north you find yourself, the more likely you are to feel the wrath of winter weather. Winter storms are "deceptive killers," according to the National Weather Service, referring to the fact that the majority of the casualties that occur are not directly related to the storm itself. People experience hypothermia from dangerously low temperatures, traffic accidents because of hazardous driving conditions, etc.

If you do not live in a location that experiences extreme winter conditions, even mild winter weather has the ability knock out power to your home, hinder communication by damaging phone lines or cell towers, and render roads impassible, leaving you unable to retrieve food and supplies. When roads cannot be accessed, it denies you the ability to evacuate to a safer area and prevents emergency vehicles from getting to your home if the need should arise.

Once you are aware of the inherent issues that come with winter storms, you can be better prepared to keep you and your family warm and safe.

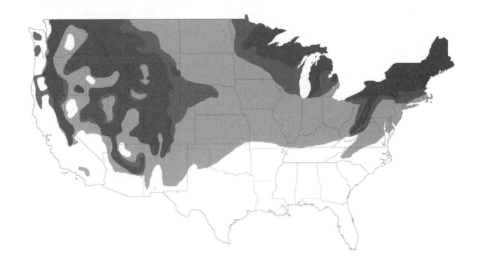

Areas of significant annual snowfall (1 to four 4) and blizzard potential in the United States. *(Source: National Oceanic and Atmospheric Administration)*

ACTIVITY 9.1: TEN PROJECTS TO PREP YOUR HOUSE FOR THE WINTER

1. Seal Your House

An easy way for cold winter air to permeate your house and for the warm inside air to escape is through the small holes and cracks that are inherent to residential construction. Caulk around all windows, doors, and all other exterior trim. Inspect the exterior of house for any penetrations where electrical outlets or plumbing enters. Silicone caulk is durable and resistant to harsh temperatures. It is commonly used for exterior applications. Latex caulk is paintable and not as odorous as silicone. It is primarily used for interior projects. There is an acrylic-latex-silicone blend caulk that is a hybrid and is considered to be the best of both worlds.

2. Have Your Furnace Inspected

Experts recommend having your furnace inspected by a licensed professional annually. An early evaluation will give you the advantage of knowing about any deficiencies before the need for your furnace arrives, which allows you time to weigh your repair/replacement options. Before winter weather arrives, make an appointment and have a thorough inspection performed to ensure that your furnace is running at its peak efficiency and, most importantly, that it's running safely.

3. Convert from Wood to Gas

There's nothing quite like the sound and smell of a wood fire burning in the fireplace. It's cozy. It's romantic. It's also inefficient and actually a pollutant. Traditional wood-burning fireplaces actually draw heat from the home and send it up the chimney. Gas fireplaces take some of the load off of your furnace and use far less energy to heat your home. They can draw air from the outside, pull it past the firebox, and send the warm air into your house.

4. Install or Check Your Carbon Monoxide Detectors

Carbon monoxide (CO) results from incomplete combustion, which can be created from a variety of sources, but most commonly your automobile and your home's gas-powered appliances. During the winter months, when furnaces and fireplaces are going strong and vehicles are left running to warm up, carbon monoxide tends to be present. Called "the silent killer," it displaces the oxygen in your blood cells and, in high doses or small doses over a long period of time, can be lethal. Because CO is tasteless, colorless and odorless there is no good way to tell if it reaches dangerous levels in your home without the help of a carbon monoxide detector.

TIPS & TRICKS

MAKE YOUR OWN CHEAP WINDOW INSULATION USING BUBBLE WRAP

Windows can be a significant source of heat loss as well as a creator of drafts in your house. One unconventional way to insulate your windows is to use bubble wrap. Bubble wrap can be purchased in large rolls and custom cut to fit your windows. You can use tape to keep it in place, or simply spray a mist of water on the glass and press the bubble wrap against it. It will stick. Bubble wrap also allows the sun's rays to carry light and heat in the room while keeping the cold out.

---

5. Protect Pipes from Freezing

Frozen water pipes can be responsible for numerous problems in your house. When the water freezes, it expands and can burst the pipe. A little bit of prevention goes a long way. To minimize the risk of frozen pipes, one simple measure can be taken: Insulate your water pipes. Most hardware stores sell foam pipe insulation wrap. It is inexpensive and can be installed by even the most inexperienced in the area of home improvement.

6. Add Insulation to Your Attic

Depending on the age of your house, there are a variety of types of insulation that could be found in your attic. Traditionally, your home will have either rolled insulation (long, wide strips of insulation that fit between the joists) or blown insulation (loose-fill insulation made from fiberglass, mineral wool or cellulose). Check the depth. Most experts recommend at least twelve inches of insulation in your attic. If you have less than that, you should add until you have an adequate depth. You will now find that there are more environmentally friendly options to insulate your attic if you decide to increase the depth.

7. Clear Branches Away from Your House

When a thick blanket of snow falls from the sky, it collects in the trees, weighing down the branches. The added weight causes branches to break and trees to fall. Unfortunately, they tend to fall on power lines and into houses, causing costly damage. By having a professional trim trees away from your house, you can minimize the chance of an unwanted hole in your house at the most inopportune time.

8. Have Your Chimney Inspected

Chimneys are made to transport smoke from the firebox of your fireplace up and out into the atmosphere. If there are cracks in the flu pipe of the chimney the embers and heated gasses coming up from your fireplace can unknowingly be finding their way into your attic. There can also be buildup of flammable material. One thing to know about smoke is that it carries soot and impurities with it. Those impurities tend to gather in the chimney's flue pipe. If you do not have it cleaned on a regular basis, that buildup can become flammable creating a fire where you don't want one. Like furnaces, chimneys should be inspected and cleaned annually.

9. Install Storm Windows

Storm windows are multiple layers of insulated glass framed in wood, vinyl or aluminum. Older single-pane glass offers minimal thermal protection and is grossly inefficient. If you have single-pane windows you should upgrade to storm windows. Storm windows can be installed relatively easily.

10. Winterize Your Outside Water Sources

Another way to prevent frozen pipes is to protect your water sources located on the exterior of your home. Remove garden hoses from the outside spigots. Shut off and drain pipes leading to outside water faucets. If you do not have individual shut-off valves for these pipes, a good warm-weather project would be to install them so you can better prepare for the cold winter weather.

KNOW YOUR LOCAL COUNTIES

It seems like a simple concept, but know the counties in which you live, work and travel. Weather warnings are issued by county name when a risk notification is made. Knowing which county you reside in and surrounding county names will give you the opportunity to heed the warnings and take action.

ACTIVITY 9.2: **BUILDING A WINTER HOME SURVIVAL KIT**

Beyond the basics that we've already addressed, winter storms present the need for special considerations in your survival kit. Hopefully by this point in the book, you already have a supply of food, water, etc. Now is the time to make sure you have what you and your family will need in the event of a cold-weather event. Make a list below of the items you will need to ensure survival and comfort for you and your family.

WINTER HOME SURVIVAL CHECKLIST

- ☐ Matches, butane cigarette lighters and stove lighters
- ☐ Fire fuel (wood, paper, etc.)
- ☐ Backup home heating methods (fuel oil, propane, solar-powered, wood-burning, etc.)
- ☐ Flashlights with batteries
- ☐ Candles
- ☐ Fire extinguisher
- ☐ Warm clothing

- ☐ Shovels
- ☐ No-power cooking method (propane, kerosene, alcohol or white gas camp stove)
- ☐ Solar charger for electronics
- ☐ Duct tape
- ☐ Tarps (and cordage to secure corners)
- ☐ Hand tools (hammer, pry bar, axe, handsaw, screwdrivers, etc.)
- ☐ Battery-operated weather radio

ACTIVITY 9.3: **BUILDING A WINTER VEHICLE SURVIVAL KIT**

Winter weather equals treacherous roads and the increased chances of being stranded. Without taking the proper precautions, being helplessly stuck in your vehicle can quickly become a life-threatening scenario.

WINTER VEHICLE SURVIVAL CHECKLIST

- ☐ Blanket(s) or four-season sleeping bag(s)
- ☐ First aid kit
- ☐ Matches, butane lighters
- ☐ Flashlight with extra batteries
- ☐ Tow rope
- ☐ Collapsible shovel
- ☐ Sand or kitty litter (for traction)
- ☐ De-icer
- ☐ Flares
- ☐ Distress flag
- ☐ Non-perishable food
- ☐ Moist wipes
- ☐ Large and small plastic bags

- ☐ Tool kit
- ☐ Compass
- ☐ Jumper cables
- ☐ Battery-operated weather radio
- ☐ Knife
- ☐ Windshield scraper and brush
- ☐ Cell phone charger (12-volt or powered by disposable batteries or solar)
- ☐ Large can and plastic cover with tissues for sanitary purposes
- ☐ Drinking water
- ☐ Snack foods, energy bars, etc.
- ☐ Small can, kettle or cooking pot (to melt snow for drinking)

TIPS & TRICKS

INSTALL CARBON MONOXIDE DETECTORS

You should have at least one carbon monoxide detector in your home. They plug into a wall outlet and have a battery back up. The most important place for a CO detector is some place that will wake you up at night. It mixes evenly with air, so even placed low into a typical wall outlet, it will still provide you with the protection you need. Prices vary (good quality detectors start in the $40 range) but a good detector, regardless of brand, will have a digital readout informing you of how many "parts per million" are in your home and what that number means to you.

WHAT TO DO (AND NOT TO DO) AT HOME DURING A WINTER STORM

1. Do monitor weather forecasts and do not travel during winter storms.

By staying aware of current and forecast weather conditions, you can avoid getting caught in most winter storms. The biggest storms can paralyze an entire region, shutting down all travel. Mountain areas, especially at higher elevations, can generate their own weather and you should be aware of the potential for isolated storms even if the overall regional forecast is good.

2. Do Check Your Preparations Before the Storm

During a winter storm, it is entirely possible that your home is unaffected, but that does not mean you shouldn't plan for the worst. If you expect to be without power and heat and plan accordingly, you will be ahead of the game when it actually happens. Review your preparations. Make sure that you have, readily available, things like flashlights and batteries or candles and lighters/matches, a battery-operated weather radio, food, water, etc. (Use the included Winter Home Survival Kit Checklist, page 151)

3. Do Not Run a Generator Indoors

Proper ventilation is required to safely operate a generator. If not, carbon monoxide can build up and cause significant medical issues up to and including death. Opening a window does not provide adequate enough ventilation and allows critical warm air to escape. Keep it outside and away from doors, windows and air vents.

4. Do Heat Just One Room in the Absence of Electricity

If you lose electricity to your home, you will have to rely on alternative ways to provide heat. Focus on a single room to heat and close off other unnecessary rooms. Seal up the room as much as possible by placing towels or blankets where warm air might be escaping under doors and, during the daytime, keep curtains or blinds open allowing in as much solar heat as possible.

5. Do Not Forget about Your Pets

In your preparations, remember to include the family pets. They will need food, water, medication, etc., just as anyone else does. They will need protection from the cold so, if possible, move outdoor pets indoors or, at the very least, to a sheltered area that will provide as much protection as possible.

6. Do Eat

In cold weather, maintaining your body temperature is paramount. One easy way to do that is to eat. Food provides fuel for the body. If possible, consume warm food, but any food will do the trick. Eating will replace the carbohydrate stores that your body uses to warm itself, as well as provide several other benefits. Consuming food will supply the nutrients essential for good health and support the ever-important psychological benefits that come along with not being hungry.

7. Do Not Overexert Yourself

Walking through deep snow, pushing a car or shoveling snow puts a significant strain on your body. It can exasperate back problems and provoke cardiac problems such as a heart attack. Avoid overexerting yourself. Take your time when walking through or working in the snow. Take frequent breaks. Dress in layers. Most importantly, do not ignore chest pain or tightness in your chest. If you experience either of those, seek medical attention as soon as possible.

8. Do Use Caution When Walking in the Snow

During a winter storm, snow accumulates on tree branches and power lines. It is common for the weight of the snow to cause tree branches to break off and fall onto power lines, or the power lines themselves to fall. Accumulated snow can easily hide a fallen power line, allowing you to unknowingly come in contact with it. Always assume a down wire is a live wire.

TIPS & TRICKS

REVERSE YOUR CEILING FAN

Most ceiling fans have a switch that will reverse the direction of the blades. Normally fans run counterclockwise, drawing the warmer air up and cooling the room. By switching the blade direction to run clockwise, the rotation of the blades will push warm air down into the room where you can feel its benefit.

WHAT TO DO (AND NOT TO DO) IF TRAVELING DURING A WINTER STORM

1. Do Stay on Main Roads and Avoid Back-Road Shortcuts

Stay on well-traveled highways and roads that are more likely to be maintained for winter travel and patrolled by emergency vehicles. Avoid secondary roads and especially remote back roads. Don't put all your trust in GPS navigation systems, as the routing information has no way of taking into account winter road conditions

2. Do Not Travel at Night If You Can Avoid It

If you must travel in winter storm conditions, try to get where you're going during daylight hours when temperatures will be higher and visibility better. Make sure you inform friends or relatives where you are going and what time you expect to be there, and provide details of the route you expect to take.

3. Do Not Let Your Fuel Tank Run Low

When traveling during the wintertime, make every effort to keep your fuel tank as full as possible. If you were to become stranded, every ounce of precious fuel may be needed to keep you alive. Obviously for longer trips keeping the tank full will be more of an effort, but the inconvenience of making frequent stops can be offset by the security of knowing that if you were to become stranded you will have given yourself as much opportunity to remain warm as possible.

4. Do Keep a Winter Survival Kit in Your Vehicle

Your chances of having an accident increase greatly when driving in winter weather conditions. With that comes the risk of becoming stranded. It is essential that you have basic supplies to keep you safe until you can get to safety or help arrives. Assemble a basic survival kit using the included Winter Vehicle Survival Checklist (page 152) and keep it in your vehicle during the winter months.

5. Do Not Leave Your Vehicle if Trapped by the Storm

If you get stuck, try to pull off the roadway if possible, turn on your hazard lights, and hang your distress flag from your antenna. Stay inside your vehicle unless you see an occupied building close by where you know you can take shelter. Even if there are multiple people in the vehicle, do not send one person to seek help. It is far too dangerous and will more than likely not end well.

TIPS & TRICKS

MYTH: THE MAJORITY OF YOUR BODY'S HEAT LOSS IS THROUGH YOUR HEAD

A popular myth is that the majority of your body's heat escapes by way of your head. There are several factors that come into play in regard to the loss of body heat: the ambient temperature, your aerobic capacity, head size, etc. The truth is that usually less than 30 percent of body heat is lost through the head. Having said that, make Mom happy. Wear a hat anyway.

---

6. Do Run the Engine for Short Periods of Heat

Run the engine and heater ten minutes each hour to keep warm. Partially open a window on the downwind side of the vehicle while running the vehicle to prevent carbon monoxide poisoning. If you are doing this in deep, accumulating snow, you should also periodically clear away snow from the exhaust pipe to prevent carbon monoxide buildup.

KNOW YOUR WINTER WEATHER TERMINOLOGY

Freezing rain—rain that falls when the surface temperatures are at or below freezing

Sleet—small pellets of ice created by frozen raindrops

Wind chill—a calculation of temperature readings and wind speed that indicates the effective temperature that you feel, which can be significantly lower than the thermometer reading

7. Do Not Remain Idle

Even in the confines of a vehicle, you should exercise frequently by vigorously moving your arms, legs, fingers and toes. Stomp your feet, clap your hands or do any other activity that will keep blood circulating and maintain body heat.

8. Do Watch for Signs of Frostbite and Hypothermia

Early recognition of cold-weather-related emergencies are vitally important. See Chapter 4 for recognition and treatment of frostbite and hypothermia.

9. Do Not Eat Snow

Avoid eating snow, if you can help it, as it will reduce your body temperature. Eating snow can actually cause your body to expend more energy to maintain a good core body temperature. The benefit of hydration is not worth the cost. Drink water and other available fluids to maintain hydration, but avoid alcohol. If you must consume snow, melt it first. In cold environments, the body's blood vessels will constrict to maintain heat. Alcohol causes the vessels to dilate, creating the illusion of warmth when, in reality, your body temperature decreases.

10. Do Make Yourself Visible After the Storm

After the storm has passed and you can safely exit your vehicle, increase your visibility to searchers by hanging a brightly colored cloth from your antenna, if it's safe to do so. You can also stomp out an SOS in the snow or arrange rocks or tree limbs to attract rescue aircraft that may be surveying the area.

PROTECTING YOUR HOME AND FAMILY AFTER THE STORM

Once the brunt of the storm has passed, there are several things you need to do as soon as it is safe to go outside again. But first, be sure to monitor local and regional weather if at all possible to make sure it is truly over.

1. If you have lost power and heat, relocate to a shelter as soon as it's safe and possible to do so.

2. Text SHELTER + your zip code to 43362 (4FEMA) to find the nearest shelter in your area (example: shelter 12345).

3. If you've lost power and it's still dark, use flashlights when possible in lieu of open flames.

4. If you suspect your water pipes have frozen, contact a plumber as soon as possible to inspect the pipes. If you know that they have frozen, shut off water to your home at the valve.

5. Check your basement for water after each snowfall. Even a small amount of water can do costly damage.

6. If you have a sump pump, clean the pit of any debris and ensure that it is working.

7. After a heavy snow, inspect your attic. The weight of snow can cause significant damage to roof structures. If rafters are broken or bent or if you hear creaking and popping, a roof collapse is possible. You should leave the attic and contact a professional to inspect and repair.

8. Remove snow from a roof by hiring a professional or using a "roof rake."

9. Ensure that downspouts are clear, allowing snowmelt to flow safely away from your foundation.

TIPS & TRICKS

UNDERSTANDING ADVISORIES, WATCHES AND WARNINGS

Winter Storm Watch—severe winter weather is possible

Winter Storm Warning—winter weather is highly likely or occurring

Ice Storm Warning—heavy accumulation of ice is expected)

Blizzard Warning—strong winds will produce blinding snow, zero visibility and life-threatening conditions

Wind Chill Warning—life threatening wind chills of -25°F or colder are expected

Wind Chill Advisory—dangerous wind chills expected of -15°F to -24°F

Winter Weather Advisory—winter weather is expected with 2 to 5 inches of snow and potentially hazardous conditions

Freezing Rain Advisory—light accumulations of ice

Chapter 10:
FIRE AND WILDFIRE

HELL ON EARTH

"It was nuclear winter. It was like Armageddon. It looked like the end of the world."
—San Diego city firefighter Mitch Mendler (2007) when asked about Southern California wildfires

Wildfires (also known as forest fires and wildland fires) start quietly, grow quickly and destroy mercilessly. Rolling infernos swallow up everything in their path without regard for life or property. Every year, millions of acres and millions of dollars in property loss are left smoldering in the aftermath of wildfires. They are possible everywhere that there is a patch of land large enough to burn.

Wildfires are immeasurably dangerous due to their sheer magnitude as well as their decisive unpredictability. Lightning strikes are a common suspect when it comes to the origin of a wildland fire, but a surprisingly low percentage of them originate that way. A thunderstorm can produce thousands of lightning strikes during its duration. While even in the presence of rain, each of them is capable of creating a fire, ground conditions have to be just right in order for ignition to occur.

The leading cause of wildfires in the United States is carelessness. A discarded cigarette, a single match, an unattended campfire or even a stray ember can ignite a catastrophic fire. With a few days of dry conditions and a moderate wind, that single small ignition source can quickly turn into a raging, out-of-control blaze.

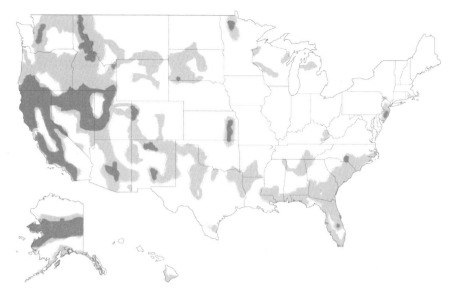

The U.S. Department of Forestry releases an annual map of predicted forest fire danger. This was the map for 2013.

UNDERSTANDING THREE PRINCIPAL FACTORS THAT DRIVE WILDFIRES: FUEL, TERRAIN AND WEATHER

FUEL

Wildfire fuels are divided up into two main categories: live and dead. Live fuels include green grass, live shrubbery and living trees. They are more prevalent during the growing seasons (sometimes called green-up periods) of spring and summer. Dead fuels are cured (dry) grasses, twigs, dead trees and layers of duff. "Duff" is the decaying leaves and branches that cover the forest floor and can contain several years of needlecast and leaf litter. The drier the dead fuel component, the more susceptible these fuels are to ignition. Chances are, regardless of where you live, that near you is a large area of wildfire fuel.

TERRAIN

The lay of the land can create wind currents that bolster already substantially burning fires. Flat terrain lacks anything to hinder the wind, allowing it to freely feed the fire. Mountainous terrain, while serving as a natural wind block, is also capable of creating a funnel effect. Terrain also has the ability to significantly impede fire crews from their suppression efforts, particularly in mountainous areas.

WEATHER

Weather can both positively and negatively affect the chance for ignition and spread of a wild-fire. Obviously, rain and snow greatly help control the potential for wildfires. Dry fuels become saturated and less likely to ignite, and at the same time they allow creeks, streams and rivers to swell, creating larger natural fire breaks. Dry and windy conditions are significant ingredients to quickly evolve a small brush fire into a free-burning wildfire.

> **TIPS & TRICKS**
>
> ### SECURE YOUR HOME BEFORE YOU LEAVE
>
> Before you evacuate (ONLY if time allows): Shut off the gas to your home, close all doors, windows, vents and fireplace flues, and remove any nearby combustibles. A few quick preventative measures could be the difference between your home becoming a victim of the fire or staying safe.

BASIC FIRE SAFETY

A wildfire is one of the few disasters where sheltering in place in your home is not an option. When you and your family are threatened by a wildfire, you must evacuate quickly—yet another reason why having a bug-out bag is so important (see Chapter 3). The key to surviving a wildfire is to not let it get close enough to put you in a race for your life that you can't win. Free-burning wildfires can spread much faster than you can run.

BECOMING FIRE CONSCIOUS

If a fire takes your home by surprise or if you're caught in the wilderness when a fire ignites, the following tips can save your life.

- **Be aware of weather and fire conditions in advance.** Awareness of your danger is the first safety measure for avoiding wildfires. Before you set out into a remote area, check with the Forest Service, Park Service or other authorities about the current fire conditions. High temperatures, low humidity and a prior period of drought that renders undergrowth tinder-dry increase the likelihood of fire and the speed at which it will spread. A chance of thunderstorms greatly increases the danger, but remember that even on a clear, sunny day, a fire can be started by a careless hiker or camper.

- **Look, listen and smell.** If you see smoke, smell smoke or hear fire, leave the area immediately. Don't waste precious time breaking camp or trying to save all your gear—just get out. The fastest escape routes will be open trails or roads where you can move unhindered by vegetation and may encounter firefighters or others who can assist you in evacuating.

- **Avoid running uphill.** Steep slopes, canyons, chutes, draws and narrow valleys act as chimneys for wildfires, which can spread in an uphill direction much faster than you can run. If caught in a mountainous area, try to work your way to a lower elevation or at least stay at the same elevation as you pick your route away from the fire. If you are at a lower elevation than the fire, your chances of outpacing it are good.

- **Retreat into water or a low spot, or dig a hole if there is time.** Larger streams, ponds, and lakes can offer a haven from fire if there is no other alternative. Get as far from the bank as possible and submerge as much of your body as you can. Be aware of the risk of hypothermia, though, as some have survived a fire, but died from overexposure in frigid water. A ditch or other natural depression, or a hole if you can dig one, can also protect you from fire and smoke.

- **Hunker down in an area with the least flammable material.** Other possible safety zones are bare, rocky areas, old burns with no new fuel, plowed fields and gravel or paved roads or other man-made clearings. If you are in a forest, be aware that evergreen trees will burn much faster than deciduous trees, and areas of undergrowth and grass will burn faster than either type of forest fuel.

- **Use jackets, backpacks, hats, blankets or other items to shield yourself from the heat.** Use anything you have with you or can find in the area to shield your body from radiant heat. Cotton or wool fabrics are best—synthetics can melt and cause severe burns. Above all, try to protect your face, neck and ears. Wrapping your hair is a good idea as well, as it can easily catch fire.

- **Stay calm; keep low and facedown to protect your airway.** If you are overtaken by the fire and forced to hunker down, try to stay calm and resist the urge to run. Your best chance of survival is to stay facedown and low to the ground, where there may be a small amount of oxygen and you can reduce the amount of smoke you inhale. The prone position also minimizes your exposure to radiant heat.

- **Burn out a safety area with an escape fire.** If you find yourself in the path of a fast-moving grass fire or brush fire with no escape route, you may be able to set an escape fire to burn out a large enough safety area. This will work only if you can start the fire quickly and if you start it in an area of highly flammable grass or brush that will burn before the wildfire reaches it.

- **Break through the fire front in to the burned out area.** Although it may result in serious burns, it is sometimes possible to survive a wildfire by passing through the leading edge into the already-burned area. Don't attempt this if the flames are more than about five feet high or deep. Move as fast as possible, and try to pick the area of least intensity while avoiding obstructions that could trip you up. As when hunkering down, try to cover your face, neck and ears.

- **Stay in your vehicle if caught by a fire while driving.** Although your instinct may be to run from your vehicle for fear of explosion, many have survived wildfires by staying inside the vehicle, which gives your body some protection from radiant heat. Get down on the floorboards and cover your head and face. Tires may deflate but gas tanks don't explode easily, and most fires will pass over before enough heat builds up for that to happen.

- **Don't return home until you're told it's safe to do so.** By coming back before authorities deem it safe, you could be putting yourself and your family in danger.

The most important things you can do in the event of a wildfire are to prepare before the event, recognize when it is happening and react quickly. Now that you know a little bit about what wildfires are, how they start and what to do about them, it's time to do some prep work. Use the following sections to identify if you live in a fire zone and to tackle a few home projects that can reduce your exposure to a wildfire. You will also find tips to help educate children about fire safety.

ACTIVITY 10.1: MAPPING YOUR FIRE ESCAPE ROUTES

Your best chance to escape a fire is to recognize the hazard and have a pre-planned route of escape, not only from your home, but from your surrounding area as well. Many unnecessary fire injuries and deaths occur due to simple lack of preparation. On the next two pages you will draw a plan for escaping a fire within your home and an evacuation route map in the event that you and your family are relocating out of the path of a wildfire. Share them with your family and practice them regularly.

TIPS & TRICKS

SELECT THE RIGHT EXTINGUISHER FOR YOU HOME

For your home fire extinguishers, it is best to use ABC extinguishers. Each letter represents a class of fire that can be extinguished: A—Common combustibles such as wood, paper, and cotton. B—Flammable liquids, and C—Electrical fires. ABC extinguishers provide the capability to extinguish all three types of fires.

Home Fire Escape Map

A common fire-safety practice is to conduct EDITH—Exit Drills In The Home. You and your family should have multiple escape routes planned from every room in your home and practice them so that everyone is familiar with the available options. On this page, you will draw a floor plan of your house. From every room in the home have a primary and secondary way to the outside. Once outside, designate a meeting place where your family can congregate to ensure that everyone escaped safely and is accounted for.

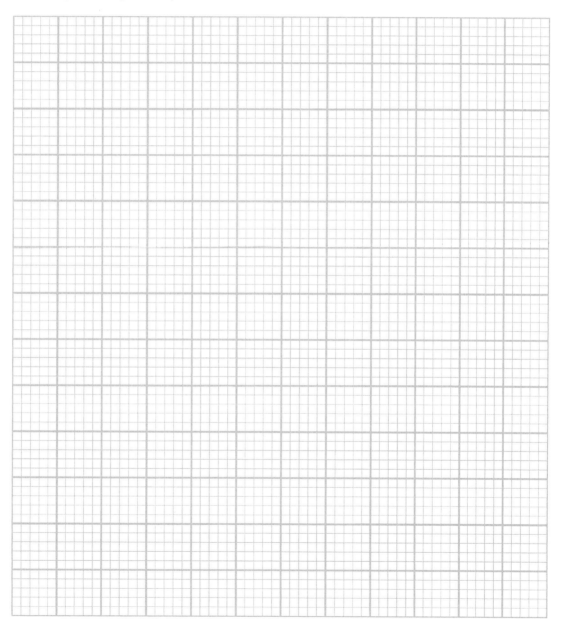

Fire Evacuation Route

In the case of a wildfire, the authorities will evacuate the area in the projected path of the blaze. This typically means that a lot of people bottleneck poplar routes trying to get to a place of refuge. On this page, paste a map of the area of the city where you live. When you decide on the best possible routes, you should select the closest and least obstructed roads; avoid trying to escape uphill, and designate multiple evacuation routes.

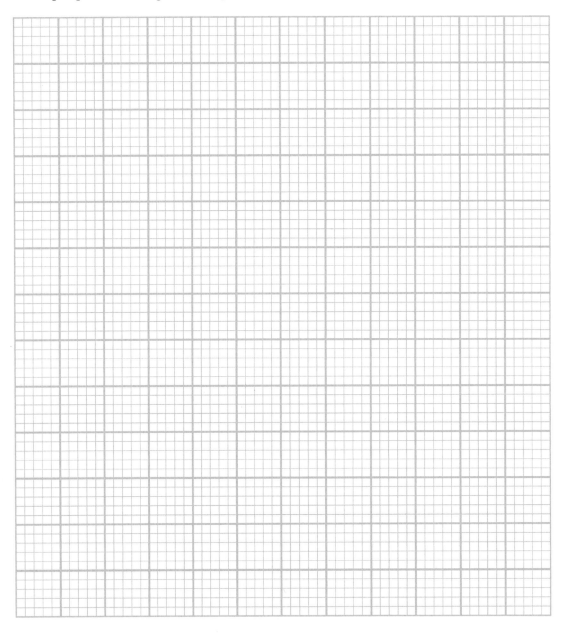

DETERMINE AND EMPLOY SKILLS WITHIN YOUR NEIGHBORHOOD

Utilize teamwork. Talk to your neighbors about wildfire safety, and plan how the neighborhood can work together if a wildfire should occur. There will be a variety of skill sets within the neighborhood. Consider how to best utilize them to help each other. Make a plan to take care of children whose parents may not be home and able to get to their kids. Pre-plan how you can assist those with special needs such as handicaps or the elderly.

ACTIVITY 10.2: HELPING YOUR HOME SURVIVE A WILDFIRE

One of the most terrifying experiences any homeowner can have is evacuating their home ahead of a wildfire and not knowing if, when they finally can return, there will be a home still standing to come back to. Firestorms can seem cruelly random, leap-frogging one house and leaving a neighbor's house perfectly intact between two piles of ash and chimney on either side. But what fire scientists and housing developers have learned from years of data is that there are plenty of ways to stack the odds in your favor. It just comes down to taking the time to fortify your home against a potential future threat. The following six simple steps could save your home:

1. Clean Your Gutters

If ignited, the combustible debris in your gutters has easy access into your attic space through vulnerable roof coverings or fascia boards. To combat this threat, install gutter guards, mesh gutter covers that allow water to adequately drain and prevent organic debris from cluttering your gutter. Regularly clean your roof and gutters to free them from leaves, pine needles, branches and other flammable materials.

2. Create a Defensible Space around Your Yome

Build a buffer between your home or building and anything that will burn—that includes grass, shrubs, trees and the woodland areas around it. A minimum of 30 feet around your house is recommended to keep clear of all dead or dry plants and vegetation, keep trees trimmed to have a minimum of 10 feet between them, and relocate woodpiles beyond the 30-foot perimeter.

3. Locate the Vents and Other Openings to Your Home (There Are More Than You Think)

If you're not familiar with construction terminology, ask someone who is about your soffit vents, through-roof vents, gable vents, ridge vents, etc. Vents are natural entry points for embers and flames. Inspect and maintain vegetation in and around the vents. Remove highly combustible plants. Clean vents regularly to avoid debris accumulation. Consider making vent covers that can be temporarily installed when a wildfire approaches your home. Vent covers can be manufactured out of inexpensive wood or any other solid substance that would provide short term protection from embers and flame.

4. Fortify Your Deck

The open space below a raised deck often accumulates combustible debris such as leaves, dead grass and weeds. Install lattice or a screen to prevent those things from collecting and creating an area of fire tinder next to your house. Stones can be utilized as ground cover beneath the deck to minimize vegetation growth.

5. Test Your Firefighting Tools on a Regular Basis

Install and ensure the readiness of the alarm and defense systems in your home: detectors and extinguishers. Install a minimum of one smoke detector and one fire extinguisher on every floor. Additional detectors placed in each bedroom are recommended, and additional extinguishers in high-risk areas such as the kitchen and garage are a good idea. Kidde is one of the more popular and reliable brands of both smoke detectors and fire extinguishers, and they can be purchased at most major department and hardware stores.

The Fire-Ready Home

1. Easy road access
2. Fire-resistant roofing
3. Clear/protected gutters
4. Fire-proof deck and patio
5. Fire-resistant landscaping
6. 30-foot fire perimeter

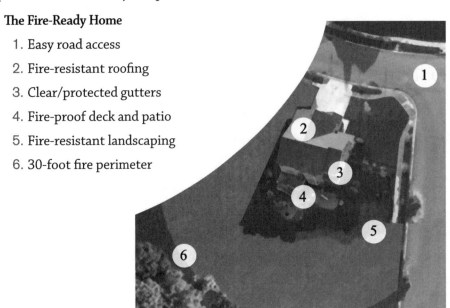

TIPS & TRICKS

APPLY WATER YOURSELF

If time allows and you can do so safely, place lawn sprinklers on your roof and aboveground fuel tanks to keep them wet and cool when threatened by heat and fire.

HOME FIRE SURVIVAL CHECKLIST

- ☐ Clean your gutters
- ☐ Clear 30 feet around your home
- ☐ Plant fire-resistant shrubs in your clearance area
- ☐ Prepare an emergency escape route
- ☐ Discuss fire safety with the family
- ☐ Have a quick evacuation bag prepared and ready
- ☐ Install smoke detectors and change batteries twice per year
- ☐ Establish a home escape plan with two exits from each room and establish a family meeting place
- ☐ Install a minimum of one fire extinguisher per floor of the home
- ☐ Keep matches and lighters out of reach of children
- ☐ Have your chimney cleaned, inspected and repaired by a professional

ACTIVITY 10.3: TALKING TO CHILDREN ABOUT FIRE SAFETY

Talking to children about fire safety is critically important. The conversations should begin when they are very young and continue as they grow. Children are naturally curious and they often see adults handling fire. We light the wood in the fireplace or the campfire. We stoke the fire and reposition the logs. We keep matches in a certain drawer to light scented candles in the house. Children see these things and don't have the experience to understand the potential damage that can be done so it is up to us to educate them.

- Discuss the uses of fire and when and why adults use it. Inform them that it can be a tool when used correctly and devastating when it isn't. Tell them the consequences of fire that isn't handled properly and how quickly careless handling of fire can get out of control. Encourage questions, and most importantly stress that any time fire is present, an adult should be present also.

- Tell children that lighters and matches are for adult use only and that if they see them to tell an adult who can relocate them to a safe place.

- Make sure they know to call 911 in case of an emergency. Tell them that if a bad situation arises to tell an adult immediately and if an adult isn't available, they are empowered to dial 911 themselves.

- If their clothing catches on fire, their instinct will be to run which only feeds the fire. They are to stop, cover their face, drop to the ground and roll until the fire is out.

- They should be taught what a smoke detector is and what it means when it activates.

- If a smoke detector activates, leave the house immediately. If their door is closed, they should feel it with the back of their hand. If there is no heat, open it to see if the house looks safe to leave through the front door. If they feel heat they should shove a blanket, towel, etc., against the bottom of the door and go to the window to shout for help.

- A child will tend to "hide" from a fire. They will hide under their bed or in a closet, which should be strongly discouraged. Know and practice the escape routes.

- Read to or have your children read to you fire safety books. There are many to choose from that are entertaining and educational, like *No Dragons for Tea*, *Big Frank's Fire Truck* and *It's Time to Call 911*. Another good book for children who have been exposed to any kind of tragedy or traumatic event is *A Terrible Thing Happened*. (See Prepper's Library on page 188 for complete book information.)

TIPS & TRICKS

KEEP THE RIGHT TOOLS ON HAND

Acquire tools that can double as protection for you home during a wildfire. Have a ladder that is capable of reaching your roof, a garden hose that can reach any and all areas of your home and other structures on your property, and maintain a cache of hand tools such as an axe, shovels, rakes, etc.

Chapter 11:
CIVIL UNREST & ACCIDENTAL & DELIBERATE MAN-MADE DISASTERS

IT'S A DANGEROUS WORLD

With a global population now exceeding seven billion people, incidents of man-made disasters of all types are inevitable and almost certain to increase in frequency and severity. Wherever large numbers of people live and work, they have the potential to create disasters of their own making that can equal or exceed the fury of many natural disasters. In this final category of potential disasters you should not overlook in your preparations, we look at human-caused events ranging from industrial accidents to deliberate acts of terrorism, and especially at the frightening destructive potential of out-of-control riots and widespread civil unrest. While some disasters of this type are totally unpredictable and almost impossible to prepare for, nevertheless there are often warning signs and indicators that tip you off to the potential for an incident to occur.

Your response will depend on the nature of the particular incident, but if you have prepared your home and family following the guidelines in this book for general preparedness and natural disaster readiness, you will likely be in good shape to deal with these human-caused disasters and survive their aftermath. Many of the same strategies and advance preparations needed for natural disasters will apply, but you should be aware of the potential for the different specific kinds of human-caused disasters that may affect your area. In the case of deliberate attacks and civil unrest, a defensive plan for your home and family will be needed as well.

ACCIDENTAL MAN-MADE DISASTERS

In today's complex and industrialized world, accidental man-made disasters can be as much of a threat as natural disasters. The possibilities cover a broad spectrum of events from chemical spills and explosions to bursting dams or even nuclear power plant accidents. It is virtually impossible to guarantee your safety against all types of man-made disasters, but being aware of the potential threats near you can help you rate the danger to your family's safety and well-being.

How many of the following potential dangers could affect your home? Check all that apply:

❑ Do you live near a chemical manufacturing plant? (Risks include explosions, contamination of local water supply or the atmosphere, sabotage or terrorist attack.)

❑ Do you live near oil or gas refineries? (Risks include explosion, fire and terrorist attack.)

❑ Do natural gas pipelines pass near your home? (Underground pipelines may be out of sight and mostly unnoticed, but they can rupture or leak and catch fire or explode in some circumstances.)

❑ Do you live near a nuclear power plant or within reach of potential fall-out downwind of one? (Nuclear power plants are well-guarded and highly regulated with safety in mind, but accidents do occasionally happen, and they could be a prime choice for an elaborate terrorist attack.)

❑ Do you live downstream of a large hydroelectric or other dam? (Dam failures can occur because of slow weakening over time due to engineering shortcomings, or can be caused by extreme weather events or earthquakes. Dams are also vulnerable to deliberate attack.)

❑ Do you live directly beneath the busy flight paths of a major airport? (The chances of an airplane crashing into your house are slim, but it does happen occasionally and you might want to give second thought to living directly under busy flight paths near the airport.)

❑ Do you live next to a busy railroad or highway where transportation accidents involving chemicals or explosives could affect your home? (Living next to a freeway, interstate highway or busy railroad could pose a risk if an accident happens nearby. Rail derailments in particular can cause large chemical spills, fires or explosions.)

After assessing the threat level from man-made disasters to your home and family, you can then determine if the risk is great enough to warrant moving elsewhere or if it is an acceptable level you can learn to live with. In the latter case, have an emergency plan and conduct drills with your family so you will be able to act quickly if an accident occurs. Pipeline companies and industrial complexes will often mail informational pamphlets outlining emergency procedures and precautions to residents living near their facilities. Be sure to read the warning information and record the phone numbers provided for reporting leaks, spills or suspect activity to the proper company and civil authorities.

TIPS & TRICKS

CULTIVATE AND MAINTAIN SITUATIONAL AWARENESS

Stay alert to potential danger and be aware of others around you at all times, especially any strange or unusual activity. Situational awareness is your best chance to avoid becoming a victim of active shooters, terrorist attacks or scenarios that quickly develop into riots.

DELIBERATE MAN-MADE DISASTERS

Since the devastating, coordinated terror attacks on the World Trade Center and the Pentagon on September 11, 2001, we have been awakened to the potential threat of deliberate man-made disasters that can equal or exceed the destruction of large natural disasters. Even before that, the Oklahoma City bombing carried out by lone terrorist Timothy McVey demonstrated the potential for mass destruction that could take place almost anywhere without warning. There is nothing you can do to guarantee your safety against such an attack, but by keeping up with what's going on in the news and being aware of potential targets nearby may give you enough of a heads-up to avoid becoming a casualty.

Types of Terror Attacks and Likely Targets

Bombs: Suicide bombers or terrorists using improvised bombs, such as in the Boston Marathon attacks or the Oklahoma City bombing, can strike anywhere, but are most likely to strike symbolic targets or crowds where they can expect to inflict the most casualties and draw the most attention to their cause.

Organized Team of Shooters: An attack such as the one that occurred in Mumbai, India, in 2008 could be the most frightening and difficult type of attack to avoid. Civilian law enforcement departments inexperienced in full-scale combat would likely be overwhelmed initially, and the casualties would be high. Such an attack could occur anywhere large numbers of unarmed people are congregated, such as sports events, concerts or festivals.

Chemical or Biological Weapons: Poisons and other deadly substances can be released into public water supplies or directly into the atmosphere with explosive devices. You can reduce the risk of being poisoned by your water by not using municipal tap water for drinking.

Lone Wolf Attacks or Deranged Active Shooter: Aside from a Mumbai-type attack, even one or two determined shooters can wreak havoc, as seen in the case of the Washington, D.C., snipers and countless school shootings and other mass shootings that have occurred in recent decades. Leave the area immediately if you hear gunshots in a public place, and stay put at home if a sniper or other shooter is on the loose in your area.

CIVIL UNREST

Civil unrest is a broad term that can encompass a wide range of dangers from human discontent and conflict. Civil unrest in the form of widespread panic, looting and violence is often an unfortunate byproduct of many of the other types of disasters covered in previous sections of this book. The simple fact is that for every person who is somewhat prepared for such events, there are many, many more who are not. The results of this can be seen time and time again, nearly every year in areas where hurricanes are frequent. Forecasters announce a storm, and though most residents know they live in a hurricane-prone area, they rush out at the last minute to sweep grocery store shelves bare in an attempt to get food and other supplies to last a few days. After a major hurricane hits, looting, armed robbery and other violent acts almost always occur in the aftermath.

But aside from these problems associated with natural disasters, civil unrest can also be sparked by political and social issues, starting quickly and escalating out of control until it involves not only the participates and law enforcement officials, but everyone in the vicinity.

AVOIDING A RIOT

An out-of-control, widespread riot can be as frightening as a storm or other natural disaster. A large crowd of angry people can become something like a monstrous, single organism, consuming or destroying everything in its path. The last place you want to be is anywhere near such a crowd. A dangerous crowd could consist of anything from excited fans at a rock concert creating a human stampede to enraged protesters armed with rifles and Molotov cocktails.

How do you avoid getting swept up in a riot or other mass violence?

1. Avoid crowded places. This is obvious, but if you live in a densely populated city, you are far more likely encounter a riot than if you live in a quiet rural area. But aside from

just being in a city, attending large gatherings such as sports events, political speeches and especially heated protests and demonstrations can greatly increase your risk.

2. Keep up with the news. Riots are often caused by economic problems, racial or political tensions, or specific events such as the outcome of a trial like the Rodney King case that sparked the Los Angeles riots of 1992.

3. Get out and stay out of disaster areas in the days and weeks to follow. Stranded and desperate survivors sometimes attack even the people who are trying to bring them relief. New Orleans, for example, almost became a war zone in the desperation that followed Hurricane Katrina. This is another reason why evacuation or bugging out may be the smartest thing to do after a big urban disaster.

4. If you see or hear signs of a riot beginning, move away from the crowd as quickly as possible. Many people will be drawn to the excitement and move closer to see what is going on. Avoid this natural human tendency and simply leave. Sticking around to find out what's going on may get you caught up in the middle of something you cannot escape.

5. Avoid bus stations, subway stations and train stations as the crowds there could panic or be swept up in the riot. In wide-scale riots or civil unrest, even airports could be swamped with desperate people trying to get out of the area.

TIPS & TRICKS

RIOTS CAN AFFECT EVERYONE

In 1992 when four Los Angeles police officers were acquitted on charges they used excessive force to subdue Rodney King when arresting him after a high-speed car chase, a six-day period of nearly citywide civil unrest and rioting occurred, beginning that evening. The violence grew in intensity, leading to looting, arson and murder. Some 2,000 people were injured and 53 killed. Over 3,600 fires were set, destroying 1,100 buildings. In addition to state and local police, 4,000 California National Guard soldiers were required to bring the situation under control.

ANALYZING CIVIL UNREST TRENDS (WHAT TO LOOK OUT FOR)

Aside from localized events that can spark almost instantaneous riots, there are general trends in society that often contribute to the potential for civil unrest on a much larger scale, perhaps even nationwide. Historical events around the globe make it clear that such civil unrest has happened often and will undoubtedly happen again, maybe someday where you live. Some of these trends that are proven contributors to discontent and violence in a society are economic recession or depression, antigovernment sentiment fueled by increasing taxes and unpopular policies, ethnic tension, class-based conflict and desire for increased political freedoms. The forms in which this civil unrest can manifest itself include protests, strikes and riots, as well as kidnappings, assassinations and terror attacks. Worldwide, in the post-WWII era, civil conflict has accounted for more deaths than conflicts between nations. In extreme cases, such conflicts lead to revolution and overthrow of the government. Usually the trends toward major discontent and violence will be clearly visible and increase slowly over time, giving you time to either leave or prepare to ride out the storm if it turns for the worst.

MOB MENTALITY

Groups of people are unpredictable, and in general the larger the group, the lower the collective IQ, as can be seen in cases where sports fans on the winning team overturn and burn police cars, break out store windows and commit other acts of rampaging violence for no logical reason. The individuals that make up the mob are cloaked in anonymity and adjust their behavior to the rest of the crowd. The mob itself, rather than the individuals that make it up, is in control.

BASIC HOME DEFENSE AND SECURITY

No matter where you live, whether in a city, small town or rural area, something could happen that could trigger unrest, rioting, looting or other potential violence that could put you and your family in danger. If you are able to see it coming, it may be best to bug out of the area in advance of these problems, but in many cases it could happen before you are aware of the problem, or other circumstances such as a natural disaster or weather that causes the problem could keep you from moving. To prepare for this possibility, you must consider how you will defend your property and protect your family if trouble comes to your door. In many cases, simply having the means and the willingness to defend your property and your family will be enough, as looters and other troublemakers will usually seek the easiest targets that offer no resistance.

To be ready for this sort of situation will require some addition preparations beyond normal home security measures designed to keep out burglars when you're away. In this kind of scenario, you will likely be facing multiple attackers bent on home invasion. When planning how you will protect your home and family in this circumstance, think in terms of how you can deter attackers from selecting your home as a target, delay those to attempt to do so and defend against those who are persistent enough to continue despite the obstacles.

The following projects will get you started with the basics of improving your home security. For a much more detailed treatment of the subject, we highly recommend getting a copy of Jim Cobb's *Prepper's Home Defense* for your home library. While some of these preventative measures may seem extreme in most normal neighborhoods, changing circumstances may make them necessary at some point. Whether you implement all the ideas or not depends on your particular situation.

A FOUR-RING HOME DEFENSE

When considering outfitting your home with personal defense measures, it's best to consider implementing a comprehensive "four-ring" approach.

Ring Four—Property Perimeter: First, begin by analyzing what you can do with the outer ring—the perimeter of your house. Do you have a substantial fence or shrub barrier capable of keeping intruders out? Simply requiring an intruder or gang of intruders to climb over a 6 to 8-foot fence, or scramble over scratchy, dense shrubs can prevent them from even making the attempt.

Ring Three—Property Plot: Next, analyze the plot of your property. There are plenty of ways to deter a person who has breached your outer ring of defense from approaching your home. Simple projects include installing solar-powered floodlights and surveillance equipment. Keep the space between your outer fence and home clear of bulky hiding places, and use low-lying shrubbery, grass or rocks in place of large bushes or outer buildings. This will allow you to pre-sight your property in the event you must defend it. Post warning signs on your property indicating that you are prepared to use force.

Ring Two—The Outside of Your Home: If the first two rings are breached, your home should stand as a fortress unto itself. Replace flimsy outer doors and windows with strong, fortified alternatives. Secure any access ways that go below your home, and clear the area immediately around your house of items that could be used to breach your windows and doors or be used to start a fire. While during a catastrophic societal collapse you can't count on the police responding to a triggered alarm, the loud noise from an installed alarm can help deter intruders from going any farther. In addition to strengthening the outside of your home, you should be prepared to physically defend your property and family. Take the time to figure out the most advantageous places to take a stand if need be, keeping in mind that elevation (upper floors) can be the strongest defensible position.

Ring One—Inside Your Home: Finally, should an intruder breach your home itself, you should be prepared to retreat to the interior. Even if you do not have a professionally constructed safe room, there are plenty of ways to fortify an interior room:

- Choose a room that has sufficient space for all the members of your family you expect to protect there. Make sure there is enough room for everyone to stand, sit or lie down comfortably. This is generally at least 7 to 8 square feet of floor space per person.

- Remove the interior wall paneling or drywall and reinforce the wall framing, doubling the studs if possible.

- Cover the interior wall framing with steel plating, followed by two layers of half-inch or three-quarter-inch plywood. You can follow this with drywall or other finishing material to make the inside look like a normal room.

- Replace the existing door with a steel door in a steel doorframe.

- Add two or three heavy-duty dead bolts so the door can be secured from the inside.

- Stock the room with the supplies you and your family will need, including food and water, blankets, pillows, flashlights and defensive weapons.

Leave the Escape Option Open: If the odds are overwhelming, be prepared to escape your home. Remember that your possessions can be replaced and homes can be rebuilt. But you only get one life and one family. Depending on your home's construction, it may be possible to incorporate a hidden escape exit from the safe room or another part of the house. In a house built on a raised foundation, for example, a hidden hatch in the floor could allow you to escape into the crawl space under the house and get out to the back or side yard while attackers are still trying to beat down the door. Have a plan in advance so that everyone in the family understands the best route out of the house and away the property.

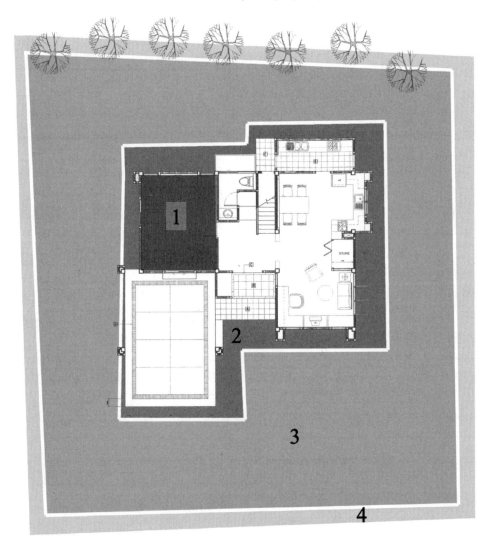

ACTIVITY 11.1: WEEKEND PROJECTS—TEN WAYS TO IMPROVE YOUR HOME SECURITY

1. **Build up your perimeter.** Start with the perimeter of your property, and if you don't have it already, consider adding either fencing or dense natural hedges such as boxwood as your first line of deterrence and delay. While even high walls will not keep out motivated invaders, they will provide obstacles that will slow down anyone approaching your house and buy you some time to retreat to a safe room or reach your defensive weapons.

2. **Install surveillance and alarm systems.** Like fences and other perimeter obstacles, these will not likely deter a gang of rampaging looters, especially if law and order has broken down and there is little chance of a police response, but they will alert you to the presence of intruders and buy you additional time to ready your defenses or move your family to a safe room.

3. **Consider temporary barricades.** Look at everything you have in and around your house and take note of what you can use for barricades against attackers if you know trouble is likely to develop. This can begin with parking vehicles across driveways or gates or moving debris, logs or other heavy obstacles into strategic positions. If there is time, you may even be able to fill and place sandbags to create barricades or fortifications. Inside your house, plan to move heavy furniture and other objects in place behind doors.

4. **Fortify your home.** Replace any exterior doors that are not made of either solid wood or steel. If there are windowpanes in the door, make solid plywood panels that can be secured over the glass from the inside, or replace the glass with heavy Lexan.

5. **Lock it up.** Install dead bolt locks on all your exterior doors if you don't have them already, and replace the short screws in your door hinges with larger, longer ones that penetrate beyond the door casing into the solid wood framing of the door opening.

6. **Replace your windows.** Swap out glass windowpanes with Lexan or cut and fit Lexan or three-quarter-inch plywood panels so that you can board up your windows from the inside if necessary. Make sure you have a means of quickly securing the panels to the window frames. An 18-volt battery-powered drill driver and a supply of large, self-tapping deck screws will make quick work of this if the window casings or framing are wood.

7. **Build a safe room.** As discussed in previous chapters, safe rooms can provide an extra layer of protection in natural disasters such as tornadoes and hurricanes. For defensive purposes, a fortified safe room can be your last-ditch retreat within the walls of your home. A safe room for such a retreat should have steel-reinforced walls

and entry-door, as well as reinforced ceilings. The idea is to make it as resistant as possible to attackers with hammers, axes or similar tools to break into.

8. **Consider getting a watch dog or a guard dog.** If you have the time and willingness to care for a full-time pet in your home, a dog can become part of your early warning system or your defensive measures, depending on breed and training. Most dogs will bark warnings at intruders and let you know someone is there. A bigger, properly trained guard dog will stop at nothing to protect its master.

9. **Build a personal armory.** Choose the firearms most appropriate for your situation, experience and skill level (see recommendations to follow). If you do not have experience, sign up for firearms safety and training courses, and make this a family endeavor. The ability and willingness to use firearms in this type of situation could be critical.

10. **Talk to your neighbors about security and defense.** Discuss possible scenarios with them and find out if you can expect cooperation and assistance in a breakdown situation where survival may depend on mutual aid. Don't forget that there is strength in numbers.

STICK CLOSE TOGETHER

If you are out in the street or other public place in a crowd that is showing signs of developing into a mob or out-of-control riot, lock elbows with your family members or friends and pick up small children until you can make your way out of the crowd's perimeter. Don't let anyone get separated from the group.

ACTIVITY 11.2: **MAPPING YOUR HOME AND PROPERTY DEFENSES**

Use this page to map out your home and property. You should use the opportunity to mark not only existing defense measures you have in place, but also defense options you would like to create in the future.

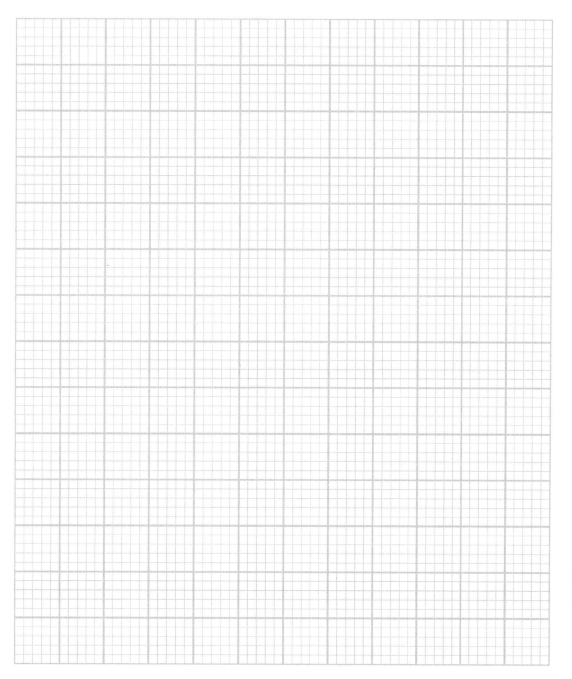

ACTIVITY 11.3: **HOME DEFENSE CHECKLIST**

PERSONAL DEFENSE CHECKLIST

- ☐ Perimeter fence or high shrubs
- ☐ Post warning signs
- ☐ Pre-sight property plot
- ☐ Replace lower window glass with heavy Lexan
- ☐ Replace flimsy outer doors
- ☐ Install additional locks
- ☐ Install solar-powered floodlights
- ☐ Build or equip a safe room
- ☐ Build a hidden escape exit if possible
- ☐ Plan to use available items on your property for barricades
- ☐ Primary home-defense firearm
- ☐ Spare magazines
- ☐ Spare ammunition
- ☐ Weapon light
- ☐ Secondary firearms for backup or other family members
- ☐ Magazines and ammunitions for secondary firearms
- ☐ Alternative weapons
- ☐ Flashlights
- ☐ Spare batteries
- ☐ Three-day water supply for each family member
- ☐ Three-day food supply for each family member
- ☐ Sleeping bags or blankets, pillows, etc., for each family member

☐ _____
☐ _____
☐ _____
☐ _____
☐ _____
☐ _____
☐ _____
☐ _____
☐ _____
☐ _____
☐ _____
☐ _____
☐ _____
☐ _____
☐ _____
☐ _____
☐ _____
☐ _____
☐ _____
☐ _____
☐ _____
☐ _____
☐ _____
☐ _____
☐ _____
☐ _____
☐ _____
☐ _____

SUGGESTED FIREARMS AND PERSONAL DEFENSE

Ultimately, defending your home and family from intruders could become a matter of life or death, and in most cases your best option for serious home defense will be a firearm of some type. Your attackers are likely to outnumber you and are likely to be armed as well. Having the right firearms and the ability to use them can be the equalizer that you need in such a situation. If you have no prior experience with firearms, however, you should not go out and purchase one without first getting proper safety instruction and training. Responsible gun owners will keep their weapons in safes or other secure locations under their control and will follow safe handling protocol. In addition, ongoing practice and advanced training is essential if you expect to prevail in an armed confrontation.

TIPS & TRICKS

MOBILITY IS KEY IN LARGE-SCALE UNREST

If long-lasting and widespread civil unrest develops, the best strategy for survival in the long run may be to leave the area completely. Time and time again, such scenarios around the globe result in long-term displacement of survivors and refugees. It's better to live to rebuild another day than remain and become a victim of a lost cause.

HUNTING AND SURVIVAL FIREARMS

If you are planning for a long-term emergency, you may choose specific firearms in advance that are the best compromise for survival and self-defense. By choosing weapons of this type you can reduce the weight of the firearms and ammo you have to carry if you end up bugging out or traveling and reduce the expense of stocking up initially. Here are some favorites in the survival category:

Semi-automatic .22 rimfire rifle: Ruger 10/22 Carbine. This .22LR carbine is a popular favorite in the category of semi-auto .22s, as it offers rugged reliability, lightweight, good accuracy and infinite potential for customization with a vast array of aftermarket parts and accessories.

Lever-action hunting rifle: Marlin 1984C. Lever-action carbines are short, lightweight and easy to handle. Chambered to handle both the .38 Special and .357 Magnum pistol cartridges, the Marlin 1894C can hold nine rounds in the magazine and is a good choice for hunting small and large game, as well as for home defense.

Pump-action shotgun: Remington Model 870. This popular shotgun is available in 12 or 20 gauge and in different magazine capacities and stock configurations for hunting or riot control or military work. Reliable pump-action shotguns are also great for general purpose survival and hunting uses because of the wide variety of ammunition available, making the suitable for everything from harvesting rabbits and game birds all the way up to stopping a charging grizzly bear.

PROPERTY DEFENSE FIREARMS

Shotguns are excellent home defense firearms that are readily available and relatively inexpensive to purchase. They are highly effective in the role of close-range defense and a good choice in dense residential environments where high-powered rifle rounds may penetrate walls and endanger people not involved. For a dedicated home defense shotgun, choose a 12-gauge riot or combat-style pump or semi-automatic shotgun with an extended tubular magazine or detachable magazines. For smaller women or children who may have trouble controlling the recoil of a 12-gauge, 20-gauge shotguns are also viable defensive weapons. Avoid pistol-grip stocks that do not also include a butt stock, as these will be difficult for anyone to aim or control.

Pump-action defensive shotgun: Mossberg 500 and 590. The Mossberg 500 series is a line of classic combat-style pump shotguns with a reputation for reliability and fast handing. These shotguns pass rigorous military-spec testing for combat use and are available in many custom configurations from the factory in addition to an array of aftermarket tactical stocks, rails and sights. The 500 holds six rounds (including one in the chamber) and the 590 holds nine.

Semi-automatic shotgun: Benelli M-4. This semi-automatic shotgun is the choice of the U.S. Marines, so it is a combat-proven weapon that will serve you well for home defense, though it is pricey compared to many pump-actions such as the Mossberg. The Benelli M-4 holds six rounds at the ready, including one in the chamber.

Semi-automatic shotgun: Saiga 12. Unlike the more common tubular magazines on most pump and semi-automatic shotguns, the 12-gauge Russian-made Saiga 12 uses detachable box magazines, making it much quicker to reload when you need more rounds. Based on the famously reliable and simple AK-47 action, this is a shotgun that offers maximum firepower. Available magazines range from 5 or 10 rounds all the way up to 12-, 20- and 30-round drums.

Semi-automatic rifles with high-capacity, interchangeable magazines offer the most firepower a civilian can own (although they are not legal in all states and jurisdictions—be sure and check your local laws). In addition to more available rounds as fast as you can pull the trigger, semi-automatic rifles and carbines also provide better accuracy and longer effective range than shotguns or handguns and are a good choice for those with larger property boundaries or in rural or semi-rural areas. There are a staggering variety of these rifles and carbines on the market and personal preferences will play a big role in selection, but here are some examples you can't really go wrong with if you are in need of this kind of weapon now:

Basic semi-automatic carbine: Ruger Mini-14. This lightweight .223-caliber carbine has been around since 1974 and had long been a favorite survival rifle as well as law enforcement weapon before the AR-15 became widely available and mostly replaced it. It is still a viable choice in a semi-automatic rifle chambered for the .223/5.56 NATO cartridge, especially if you want a weapon with a lower profile that will attract less attention than the popular "black" rifles.

Semi-automatic M4-clone or AR-15: Colt LE 6920. There are many civilian versions of the M4 or AR-15, but this particular Colt model is about as close as you can get to a military-spec M4 (though only in semi-automatic, of course). A quality AR-15 offers great accuracy as well as compact size and light weight, and the ability to use standard 30-round magazines allows great firepower in a small package.

Semi-automatic AK-47 variants: Like the AR-15, there are lots of choices when it comes to semi-automatic versions of the famous AK-47. Cheaper versions are assembled from mismatched surplus parts and can be found for a few hundred dollars. Higher-quality rifles such as those made by Arsenal are more expensive, but well worth it if you don't mind the price. Saiga sporting rifles imported new from Russia are also of good quality and can easily be converted back to the standard AK-47 configuration using standard 30-round magazines.

SIG Sauer 556R: Chambered for 7.62x39mm and using AK-47 style magazines, this carbine comes ready-equipped with a folding stock that reduces overall length to 26 inches. Though similar in many ways to the AK-47, the 556R is a thoroughly modern rifle that has attracted many serious shooters who want something a little more refined than the often-rough imported versions of the AK.

TIPS & TRICKS

OPENING A CAN WITHOUT A CAN OPENER

In the urban environment, foraging for food will likely involve scrounging around for stashes of long-lasting canned goods. If you don't have a can opener, you can still open a can neatly and safely by turning it upside down and abrading the rim by rubbing it vigorously back and forth over a flat concrete surface. The concrete will cut through the seal, then you can turn the can back right side up and squeeze the sides to pop the lid off.

PERSONAL DEFENSE FIREARMS

Handguns for personal protection offer all the advantages of small size that makes them easy to conceal and carry, increasing the odds that you will have the weapon with you when you need it. This is especially true of the smaller designs made specifically for concealed carry. Full-sized handguns fit easily in your bug-out bag and can serve as home defense weapons as well, though with some limitations compared to shotguns and rifles.

Compact concealed-carry revolver: S&W M&P 340. This compact revolver with an integral hammer that won't snag on clothing when you draw it is an easy to carry, easy to conceal package that will fit in your pocket. It only holds five rounds in the cylinder, but should do the job in a close encounter, chambered for .38 Special +P or .357Magnum.

Compact concealed-carry pistol: Ruger LC380. Lots of manufacturers offer small, semi-automatic pistols in smaller calibers than standard combat or service pistols. The Ruger LC380 is a reliable choice in this kind of pocket-sized pistol. Chambered for .380 ACP with a capacity of 7 +1, it could be a good choice as a backup to a full-sized handgun or your rifle or shotgun.

Full-sized combat-style semi-automatic pistol: Glock 17 or 21. Glock pistols have the combat-proven reputation to go "bang" every time you pull the trigger and are a top choice of law enforcement and military units around the world. They are simple, easy to maintain and reasonably priced. The Glock 17 is chambered for 9mm with 17-round magazines. The Glock 21 is chambered for the .45 ACP and uses 13-round magazines.

Full-sized revolver: Ruger GP100 .357 Magnum. A full-sized, double-action revolver chambered in a magnum caliber like the .357 can be a good choice if you need a handgun that can serve for defense against dangerous animals as well as humans (go with at least a .44 Magnum though if you expect to encounter large bears). With adequate barrel length and sight setup, such a handgun can also serve as a weapon for survival hunting. For the money, you can't go wrong with the rugged Ruger GP100 in stainless steel.

TIPS & TRICKS

MARTIAL ARTS TRAINING

Learning basic self-defense techniques may save your life in a situation where you need to quickly get out of a crowd or other danger zone. Learn to get out of various holds and restraints, defend against kicks and punches, and use movement and footwork to avoid or minimize the effect of a personal attack. To be effective, the martial art you choose to study should focus on modern hand-to-hand combat rather than sport competition or tradition.

PEPPER SPRAY FOR SELF DEFENSE

Pepper spray can be a great non-lethal weapon to aid your escape from a crowd or multiple-attacker situations. When choosing defensive sprays, be sure and get spray with oleoresin capsicum (OC) as the main ingredient, with a minimum of 10 percent. The purpose of pepper spray is not to completely disable an attacker, but to keep them away from you and allow you to escape. It is one of the least expensive and easiest to use forms of protection available, and since it comes in small containers, is easy to conceal and carry.

ALTERNATIVE DEFENSE WEAPONS

Alternative defensive weapons can include fighting knives, fighting staffs, Escrima sticks or other martial arts weapons, as well as non-lethal defensive measures such as pepper spray or electroshock weapons. Knives and other serious hand-to-hand combat weapons can be a great alternative or backup to firearms, but only if you have proper training and experience in their use. It is far too easy for your opponent to take them away from you and use them against you if you do not. For those without this kind of specialized training, pepper sprays, stun guns or tasers are a good alternative.

Pepper spray: Inferno, by Cold Steel. This combination of 8 percent oleoresin capsican and 2 percent black pepper is designed to dissolve into liquid on contact and completely incapacitate the most determined attacker.

Stun guns: Stunmaster stun gun. Offered in different sizes and voltage outputs, these compact stun guns are easy to conceal and carry, and inexpensive to buy and maintain. Stun guns are close proximity weapons that deliver an electric shock on contact. Unlike pepper sprays and tasers, they do require you to make contact with your assailant.

Tasers: Taser C2 Gold Kit. Tasers give you the advantage of distance, with a range of up to 15 feet, but you must hit your target with the two probes to be effective. The Taser C2 Gold Kit comes with two live cartridges and a training cartridge for practice. Tasers are in the price range of some handguns and are also regulated and restricted in many areas. Check your local laws before considering this option.

SAFETY FIRST

It is essential to keep your firearms safely stored in a way that you have access to them when you need them, but your children or their friends or other visitors in your house cannot get to them. Simply hiding firearms is never enough, especially if there are small, curious children in the home. If you have children too young to understand firearms, at a minimum you need to keep your weapons unloaded, with the ammunition and magazines stored separately and out of reach. Better yet, install trigger locks or locking cables on the slide mechanisms or keep the firearms locked in a gun safe with the keys hidden. When your children are old enough to understand the responsibility, they should be taught safe handling and use of the firearms in your household. But even if you do this and everyone in the family is trained and drilled in firearm safety, it is still a good idea to purchase a gun safe to secure your weapons while you are away.

ADDITIONAL READING

Armed Response: A Comprehensive Guide to Using Firearms for Self-Defense

Combat Shooting with Massad Ayoob

The Gun Digest Book of Concealed Carry

Facing Violence: Preparing for the Unexpected

Complete Krav Maga: The Ultimate Guide to Over 230 Self-Defense and Combative Techniques

Tao of Jeet Kune Do

Living the Martial Way: A Manual for the Way a Modern Warrior Should Think

---

ACTIVITY 11.3: CONDUCT A HOME DEFENSE DRILL

Just as with tornadoes, earthquakes and other natural disasters, you can better prepare your entire family for home defense by conducting drills to ensure that everyone knows what to do and where to go in case of an attack.

1. Announce the "event" that has happened make sure everyone in the household knows that looters, rioters or other attackers may be moving into the neighborhood.

2. Close outside gates, move vehicles or other temporary barricades you plan to use outdoors, and activate alarm and surveillance systems if they are not already on.

3. Lock exterior doors and windows, adding barricades, boarding and other layers of defense that are part of your planning.

4. Move into your safe room and/or ready defensive weapons and ammunition, making sure everyone follows safety procedures that should have already been part of your training.

5. After the drill, discuss the "what-ifs?" of various scenarios and what could have gone wrong and what each of you could do better in preparing for defense.

TALK TO YOUR CHILDREN ABOUT DEFENSIVE PREPARATIONS

Make sure your children understand the kinds of threats you are preparing for and why you need things like firearms in the house. Just as your would probably rather not scare them with talk of tornadoes, earthquakes, fires and hurricanes, you might prefer not to have to worry them with the possibility of riots and terrorist attacks. But in order to keep them safe, they need to understand that we live in a dangerous world and they need to know what to do when the worst happens. Just keep the level of detail age appropriate, and most kids will be able to handle this information without being unduly frightened.

Appendix

THE PREPPER'S LIBRARY: RECOMMENDED READING

"Know where to find the information and how to use it. That's the secret of success."
—Albert Einstein

No amount of information is enough when it comes to survival and keeping your family safe. Because the knowledge that is available to you is virtually limitless, you should learn as much as you possibly can and keep some books on hand that you can refer to when the need should arise. We've compiled some books to get you started.

Prepping and Survivalism Books

Bradley, Arthur T. *Preppers Instruction Manual: 50 Steps to Prepare for Any Disaster*. CreateSpace Independent Publishing Platform, 2012.

Carr, Bernie. *The Prepper's Pocket Guide, 101 Easy Things You Can Do to Ready Your Home for a Disaster*. Berkeley, CA: Ulysses Press, 2011.

Cobb, Jim. *The Prepper's Complete Book of Disaster Readiness: Life-Saving Skills, Supplies, Tactics and Plans*. Berkeley, CA: Ulysses Press, 2013.

Cobb, Jim. *Prepper's Home Defense: Security Strategies to Protect Your Family by Any Means Necessary*. Berkeley, CA: Ulysses Press, 2012.

Larsen, Matt, Department of U.S. Army. *U.S. Army Survival Handbook*, Revised. Guilford, CT: Morris Book Publishing, LLC, 2009.

Layton, Peggy. *Emergency Food Storage and Survival Handbook: Everything You Need to Know to Keep Your Family Safe in a Crisis*. Roseville, CA: Prima Publishing, 2002.

Ludwig, Art. *Water Storage: Tanks, Cisterns, Aquifers and Ponds for Domestic Supply, Fire and Emergency Use*. Santa Barbara, CA: Oasis Design, 2005.

Rawles, James Wesley. *How to Survive the End of the World as We Know It: Tactics, Techniques, and Technologies for Uncertain Times*. New York: Penguin Group, 2009.

Storey Wisdom's Country Wisdom Boards, eds. *Country Wisdom & Know-How*. New York: Black Dog & Leventhal Publishers, Inc., 2004.

Wiseman, John "Lofty." *SAS Survival Handbook, Revised Edition: For Any Climate, In Any Situation*. New York: William Morrow Paperbacks, 2009.

Prepping Books by Author Scott B. Williams

Bug Out: The Complete Plan for Escaping a Catastrophic Disaster Before It's Too Late. Berkeley, CA: Ulysses Press, 2010.

Bug-Out Vehicles and Shelters: Build and Outfit Your Life-Saving Escape. Berkeley, CA: Ulysses Press, 2011.

First Aid and Survival Medicine

Alton, Joseph and Amy Alton. *The Survival Medicine Handbook: A Guide for When Help is Not on the Way*. Doom and Bloom LLC, 2013.

Craig, Glen K. *U.S. Army Special Forces Medical Handbook*. Boulder, CO: Palàdin Press, 1988.

Dickson, Murray. *Where There Is No Dentist*. Berkeley, CA: Hesperian Foundation, 2009.

Handal, Kathleen A., American Red Cross. *The American Red Cross First Aid and Safety Handbook*. The American Red Cross, 1992.

Werner, David, Carol Thuman and Jane Maxwell. *Where There is No Doctor*. Berkeley, CA: Hesperian Health Guides, 2013.

Practical Cookbooks, Hunting & Food Storage

Ashworth, Suzanne, David Cavagnaro and Kent Whealy. *Seed to Seed: Seed Saving and Growing Techniques for Vegetable Gardeners, 2nd Edition*. Decorah, IA: Seed Savers Exchange, 2002.

Bubel, Mike and Nancy Bubel. *Root Cellaring: Natural Cold Storage of Fruits and Vegetables*. North Adams, MA: Storey Publishing, 1991.

Eastman, Wilbur F. *A Guide to Canning, Freezing, Curing, & Smoking Meat, Fish & Game*. North Adams, MA: Storey Publishing, 2002.

Languille, Julie. *Meals in a Jar: Quick and Easy, Just-Add-Water, Homemade Recipes*. Berkeley, CA: Ulysses Press, 2013.

Marianski, Stanley, Adam Marianski and Robert Marianski. *Meat Smoking and Smokehouse Design*. Bookmagic, LLC, 2009.

Markham, Brett L. *Mini Farming: Self Sufficiency on ¼ Acre*. New York: Skyhorse Publishing, 2010

Mettler, John J. *Basic Butchering of Livestock & Game*. North Adams, MA: Storey Publishing, 2003.

Nestor, Tony. *The Modern Hunter-Gatherer: A Practical Guide to Living Off the Land*. Flagstaff, AZ: Diamond Creek Press and Ancient Pathways, LLC, 2009.

Pennington, Tess. *The Prepper's Cookbook: 300 Recipes to Turn Your Emergency Food into Nutritious, Delicious, Life-Saving Meals*. Berkeley, CA: Ulysses Press, 2013.

Thayer, Samuel. *The Forager's Harvest: A Guide to Identifying, Harvesting and Preparing Edible Wild Plants*. Ogema, WI: Forager's Harvest, 2006.

Geographic and Weather Reference Material

Dunlop, Storm. *The Weather Identification Handbook: The Ultimate Guide for Weather Watchers*. Guilford, CT: Lyons Press, 2002.

Ludlum, David. *National Audubon Society Field Guide to North American Weather*. New York: Alfred A Knopf, 1991.

Rand McNally 2014 Road Atlas United States, Canada, & Mexico. Skokie, IL: Rand McNally, 2013.

Watts, Allen. *Instant Weather Forecasting*. 4th ed. Sheridan House, 2012.

Books for Children

Carr, Bernie. *Jake and Miller's Big Adventure: A Prepper's Book for Kids*. Berkeley, CA: Ulysses Press, 2014.

Holmes, Margaret M. and Sasha J. Budlaff. *A Terrible Thing Happened*. Washington, D.C.: Magination Press, 2000.

It's Time to Call 911: What to Do in an Emergency. Carlsbad, CA: Penton Overseas, Inc. 2005.

McGuire, Leslie. *Big Frank's Fire Truck*. New York: Random House Books for Young Readers, 1996.

Pendziwol, Jean E. *No Dragons for Tea: Fire Safety for Kids (and Dragons)*. Tonawanda, NY: Kids Can Press, 1999.

IMPORTANT WEBSITES AND CONTACT NUMBERS

Weather and Disaster Information Websites

Disaster Information: www.fema.gov

Flooding: www.floodsmart.gov

National Hurricane Center: www.nhc.noaa.gov

National Weather Service: www.weather.gov

Storm Prediction Center: www.spc.noaa.gov

Wildfires: activefiremaps.fs.fed.us

Important Phone Numbers

U.S. Coast Guard: 911 or VHF-FM Channel 16 (156.8 MHz)

FEMA Contact: 1-800-621-FEMA (3362)

Poison Control: 1-800-222-1222

Red Cross: 1- 800-RED (733)-CROSS (2767)

Salvation Army: 1-800-SAL (725)-ARMY (2769)

Suicide Prevention: 1-800-273-TALK (8255)

Prepping Information Websites

American Preppers Network: www.americanpreppersnetwork.com

The Apartment Prepper: www.apartmentprepper.com

Bug-Out Survival: www.bugoutsurvival.com

The Daily Prep: www.thedailyprep.com

SHTF Blog: www.SHTFblog.com

Survival Blog: www.survivalblog.com

Survival Cache: www.survivalcache.com

Survival Common Sense: www.survivalcommonsense.com

The Survival Doctor: www.thesurvivaldoctor.com

The Survival Mom: www.thesurvivalmom.com

Survival Weekly: www.survivalweekly.com

Smartphone Apps

Reliance on technology can be dangerous without the knowledge and skills to provide the foundation to survive without it. When it is available we have the advantage of virtually limitless resources at our fingertips. Below are some examples of smartphone apps that can provide with you with life-saving information, reference material or tools for navigation, communication, data storage and other critical needs.

Android and iPhone Apps

- Backcountry Navigator
- Disaster Alert
- Disaster Readiness
- Dropbox
- Earthquakes
- E-food Storage
- Evernote
- FEMA
- Floodwatch
- Google Earth
- Google Maps
- Hurricane Express
- iMap Weather Radio
- iNavX
- Kindle

- Life 360
- National Hurricane Center
- NOAA Buoy and Tide Data
- NOAA's National Weather Service
- Pet First Aid
- Pocket First Aid
- Pocket First Aid & CPR
- Quakefeed
- Red Cross (Tornado, Hurricane, Earthquake, Wildfires, Shelter View)
- Red Panic Button
- SAS Survival Guide
- Skype
- Stormtracker
- The Weather Channel

STANDARD CONVERSION CHARTS

Measure	Equivalent	Metric
1 teaspoon	—	5 milliliters
1 tablespoon	3 teaspoons	14.8 milliliters
1 cup	16 tablespoons	236.8 milliliters
1 pint	2 cups	473.6 milliliters
1 quart	4 cups	947.2 milliliters
1 liter	4 cups + 3½ tablespoons	1000 milliliters
1 ounce (dry)	2 tablespoons	28.35 grams
1 pound	16 ounces	453.49 grams
2.21 pounds	35.3 ounces	1 kilogram
100°F / 200°F / 350°F	—	38°C / 93°C / 175°C

RELIEF MAP OF THE UNITED STATES

- [ ] _____
- [ ] _____
- [ ] _____
- [ ] _____
- [ ] _____
- [ ] _____
- [ ] _____
- [ ] _____
- [ ] _____
- [ ] _____
- [ ] _____
- [ ] _____
- [ ] _____
- [ ] _____
- [ ] _____
- [ ] _____
- [ ] _____
- [ ] _____
- [ ] _____
- [ ] _____
- [ ] _____
- [ ] _____
- [ ] _____
- [ ] _____
- [ ] _____
- [ ] _____
- [ ] _____

- [ ]
- [ ]
- [ ]
- [ ]
- [ ]
- [ ]
- [ ]
- [ ]
- [ ]
- [ ]
- [ ]
- [ ]
- [ ]
- [ ]
- [ ]
- [ ]
- [ ]
- [ ]
- [ ]
- [ ]
- [ ]
- [ ]
- [ ]
- [ ]
- [ ]
- [ ]
- [ ]
- [ ]
- [ ]
- [ ]

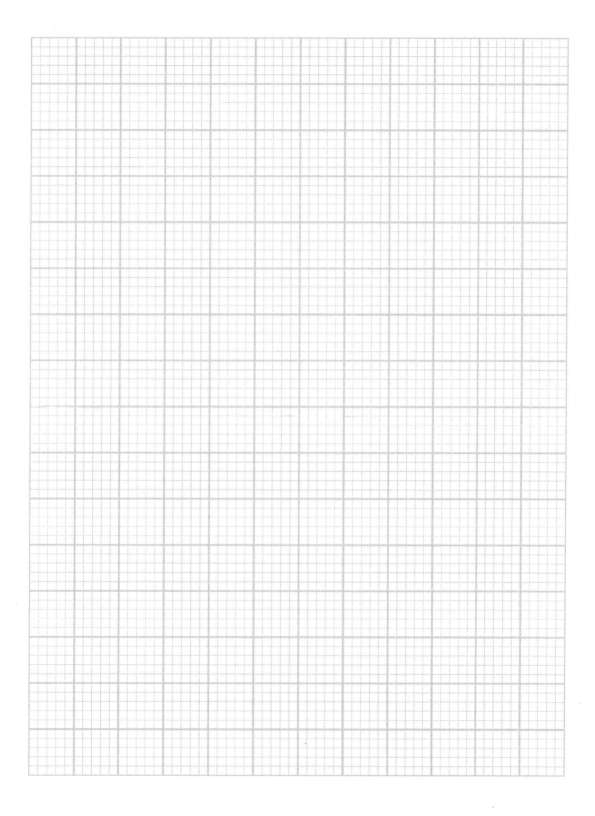

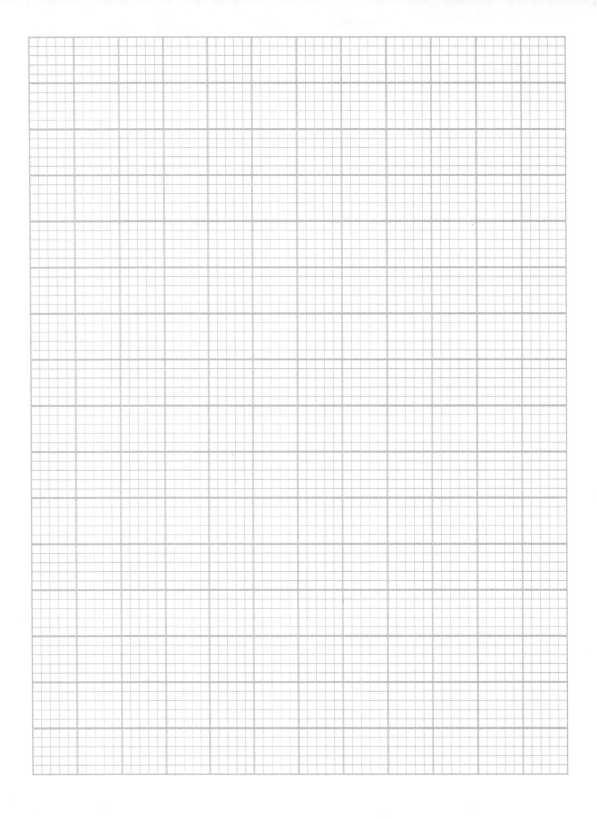

FAMILY MEMBER INFORMATION SHEET

Full legal name: _____

Date of birth: _____

Place of birth: _____

Height: _____

Weight: _____

Eye color: _____

Hair color: _____

Physical description: _____

_____

_____

_____

PASTE PHOTO HERE

Date of photo: _____

Address: _____

_____

_____

Phone number: _____

E-mail: _____

SSN (optional): _____

Fingerprints/DNA sample (optional)

Personal Medical Information

Primary doctor: _____

Phone: _____ Blood type: _____

Allergies: _____

Medical conditions: _____

_____

_____

Medications: _____

_____

_____

Notes: _____

FAMILY MEMBER INFORMATION SHEET

Full legal name: _____

Date of birth: _____

Place of birth: _____

Height: _____

Weight: _____

Eye color: _____

Hair color: _____

Physical description: _____

_____

_____

_____

PASTE PHOTO HERE

Date of photo: _____

Address: _____

_____

_____

Fingerprints/DNA sample (optional)

Phone number: _____

E-mail: _____

SSN (optional): _____

Personal Medical Information

Primary doctor: _____

Phone: _____   Blood type: _____

Allergies: _____

Medical conditions: _____

_____

_____

Medications: _____

_____

_____

Notes: _____

IMAGE CREDITS

All images from Shutterstock.com

page 7 © Bukhavets Mikhail

page 11 © cox design

page 12 © Ivancovlad

page 34 © Sura Nualpradid

page 69 © Jorge Hackeman

page 89 © Wellphoto

page 105 © Fedor Selivanov

page 109 © banderlog

page 110 © Solarseven

page 119 © B747

page 129 © northallertonman

page 139 © IrinaK

page 147 © Igumnova Irina

page 158 © art-pho

page 169 © bibiphoto

page 192 © AridOcean

ACKNOWLEDGMENTS

Scott B. Williams: I would especially like to thank Keith Riegert for bringing his vision and publishing expertise to this project, resulting in a far more useful and informative book than the simple compilation of checklists I originally conceived. Keith and the rest of the staff at Ulysses Press, especially the interior designers, have put a tremendous effort into organizing and presenting the information contained in these pages in the most logical and practical manner. Scott Finazzo has likewise brought an entirely new dimension to the project with his extensive real-world emergency and disaster experience. Thanks Scott, for all your hard work and for trusting my navigation and judgment enough last summer to sail with me across the Gulf of Mexico on a boat you'd never seen! Thanks also to Jim Cobb, for endorsing our effort to help others prepare with his message to our readers in the foreword. And once again, to Michelle, for keeping me on track with the support, understanding and love I'd be lost without.

Scott Finazzo: I would like to thank everyone at Ulysses Press, particularly Acquisitions Editor Keith Riegert for his diligent work in seeing this project come to life. Scott B. Williams for bringing me aboard and for his mentorship and friendship. Ryan, Nick and Cameron Finazzo for always being the reason why. Amy Finazzo for providing an often thankless and unwavering support system, for which I will always love you and am forever grateful. To my parents, brothers, sisters, extended family and friends for the support and having my back—you're the best! My OPFD family. And Greg Barnes at Fireside BBQ for the storm shelter.

ABOUT THE AUTHORS

© Michelle Cleveland

Scott B. Williams has been writing about his adventures for more than twenty-five years. His published work includes dozens of magazine articles and ten books, with more projects currently underway. His interest in backpacking, sea kayaking and sailing small boats to remote places led him to pursue the wilderness survival skills that he has written about in his popular survival books such as *Bug Out: The Complete Plan for Escaping a Catastrophic Disaster Before It's Too Late* and *Bug-Out Vehicles and Shelters: Build and Outfit Your Life-Saving Escape*. He has also authored travel narratives such as *On Island Time*, an account of his two-year solo sea kayaking journey through the Caribbean. With the release of *The Pulse* in 2012 and *The Darkness After* in 2013, Scott moved into writing fiction and has plans for many more novels in the future.

His current work in progress at the time of this printing is a sequel to *The Pulse*, scheduled for publication in the summer of 2014. More information about Scott can be found on his main website: www.scottbwilliams.com.

© Nick Finazzo

Scott Finazzo has been a professional firefighter for over fifteen years and is currently serving as a Lieutenant for the Overland Park (Kansas) Fire Department. He and his family live in Kansas, where Scott has been writing in various capacities for much of his life. With years of experience both preparing for and responding to disasters, he has developed a keen interest in survival. His self-reliance skills have been honed by journeying into places such as the Rocky Mountains and several islands throughout the Caribbean. Scott maintains an intrinsic connection to travel and adventure, documenting many of his endeavors on his blog: www.lureofthehorizon.tumblr.com.

Scott's next book, *Why Do All the Locals Think We're Crazy?*, which chronicles his kayak foray through the Virgin Islands, will be available in the summer of 2014. Learn more at www.scottfinazzo.com.